This is Not for You

a Memoir

Venus Soileau

Carver, Jolie, and Rory, you are my world. Moo and Poppa—thank you.

Jared, what a ride.

Contents

Author's Note

The events I have written about took place some time ago. I have recreated the events, locals and conversations from my memories of them. In the interest of protecting the privacy of individuals I have changed their names. Time elements have been condensed for the sake of narrative flow. This is a collection of my memories.

Preface

This is the 10th anniversary of the original publication of this story. I swore I would never crack the spine of this book again once it was published. I lived it, I told it, but as the years passed I realized I had more work to do. My hope is for this book to continue to start conversations that will create connections.

Just as nothing can bring me back to that time, nothing can erase it from my being. My past has made me resilient; it is perhaps the greatest gift to come out of this. I hope my children and anyone gracious enough to read this will take away the idea that anything is possible. Be kind to others, but understand the importance of self-preservation.

The adults in my life struggled with addiction and untreated mental illness. Unfortunately, that combination can set off a chain of unimaginable events. Reflecting on my relationships through the years, I am reminded of how decisions drastically and unintentionally change the lives of those you love.

I have portrayed the people in this memoir as my memory recalls them. This is my story. As I wrote, I reminded myself that my purpose was solely to narrate my story. If, through telling it, I can inspire change or help someone overcome the seemingly impossible, that would be more than I could ever ask for. In sharing my experiences I hope to create a sense of connection for others. A simple human connection can guide us at our weakest moments.

Part 1

Chapter 1

I was a little thing, sitting on a shiny porcelain toilet with my silk panties dangling around my ankles. I shouted; I was done. Waiting for my mom to come in. When my grandmother "Maw-maw" walked in, she announced Mom was gone. Even then, I knew that "gone" meant "not coming back anytime soon." Not dead gone, just not around. Mom left me to live with her parents around my first birthday. I heard stories my entire life about how my parents eventually split. My mom rambled on and on about how my dad's drug habit led him to beat her. My dad would recall my mom's mental instability and how her drug habit drove him crazy. My parents lived in Texas until my mom left him, and I ended up with my grandparents in Louisiana. Mom would pop in from time to time and visit me but always went back to her own life. Eventually, I got used to the routine.

By the time I was in kindergarten, my grandfather—"Paw-paw," as I called him—woke up each day and went to work. When he came home, we ate our evening meal, and I sat at the table, crying, while he made me practice reading *See Dick and Jane Run*. His head was shiny and bald—his friends called him Slick. Weekends were spent at Padnah's, a dance-and-bingo hall. That was the highlight of the weekends back then. My Maw-maw would rake a brush through my hair, pulling it back tight against my scalp, tugging up the corners of my eyes. She hated fixing my hair but would never cut it.

Sometimes I think she pulled that brush through a little harder than it needed as she cursed in Cajun French, "fit-putain" ("son of a bitch")—not to hurt me but to let the world know of her hardships. Dressed in our Sunday best, we were off. I'll never forget the drive through the country roads of St. Martinville. Long winding roads lined sugarcane fields swaying in the breeze. Maw-maw, popping her Wrigley's Spearmint gum, my Paw-paw casually let his arm hang out of the window, and a lit Marlboro Red dangled from his mouth. Aunt Cara, their youngest daughter, sat against the door of the back seat. My face pressed against the window, trying to keep count of the rows of the sugarcane fields as they whizzed by, looking like a mammoth fan to me.

The ride there was uneventful, making my eyelids heavy in the heat. Sitting during bingo for hours was not easy for a seven-year-old. I knew better than to run around and play like the other kids; Maw-maw didn't have to tell me not to move. I sat for hours, waiting for someone to give me something to do. Occasionally, a fat old lady whose breath smelled of decay would ask me if I could watch her cards while she went to the bathroom. That was the only time I moved, when an adult instructed me to. That usually earned me a quarter or a cherry Coke, not the cherry Coke you buy already mixed, but a real cherry Coke. I loved going to the bartender and watching him mix it up for me. He'd grab a bunch of cherries with shiny tongs and drop them right on top of my fizzing soda. Followed by a stream of cherry juice from the jar. If things were going well at the Bourré (a Cajun card game) table in the back room, my Paw-paw would hoist me up on his hip and carry me in as if I were his human good-luck charm. The smoke was so thick my eyes watered, but the thought of complaining never occurred to me; this was sacred ground, a privilege. Proud I'd sit on his lap and watch.

Each adult had a cigar box in front of them. No one wanted their money on the table in plain view. When Paw-paw tossed his ante, he slammed his knuckle on the table. When he won, everyone was happy. If my Maw-maw won, we were giddy. The ride home was long if they lost at the card table and bingo. Driving back was naturally dark, but the air in the car grew heavy. On a losing night, my Paw-paw swerved more than a little. My Maw-maw cursed him in French as she jabbed her foot at the imaginary brake pedal, frantically grasping the dashboard as if she could steer the car with her bare hands—more than once, she recited the "Our Father" all the way home to New Iberia. Somehow, we always made it back.

Like my mother, my uncle often left his children, to be tended to by my Maw-maw. Our parents just seemed busy doing their own thing. One day, as we sat in the living room, my baby cousin was walking around and running back and forth from the wooden rocking chair to the couch, giving everyone big wet kisses as his saggy diaper flopped behind him. He fell behind the rocker that day, and the wood sliced his eyebrow open. I had never seen so much blood, except when I peeked between my fingers when I wasn't supposed to and saw blood gushing down the hall from a scene in a scary movie.

I was frozen in fear. My Maw-maw ran around cursing in French while my Paw-paw smashed a rag to his brow. Within seconds, we were piled into the car while my cousin wailed. When we pulled up in a strange dirt driveway, chickens and roosters ran everywhere as if the sky was falling. An old man stood in the doorway, neither black nor white, just wrinkled up. As my cousin was carried up the steps everyone rambled in Cajun French as I pretended to understand every word. A man laid my cousin on his wooden table, and he began reciting chants in French while holding a butter knife to the brow of my baby cousin. That's how we were tended to in emergencies by traiteurs, Cajun doctors. Eventually there was no more blood. We drove home as my cousin babbled in his sleep.

Fishing was something we did often. By the time I was seven, I could bait my hook and cast my line as well as any adult. Our fishing spot was down an old country road.

Maw-maw always went off on her own. Not only go off, but she'd be standing in the marsh with cattails and weeds taller than her. She always carried a wet washcloth. In tow, she packed a white porcelain bucket we used to pee or vomit in if the urge struck us in the car. I remember how my grandpa would curse while she trailed off into the marsh. "Marie, I don't want to hear it when you get bitten by an alligator."—he shook his head, bent down, baiting his line. Fishing was relaxing. On our way back, he would pull off on a side road and stop. We knew what to do. We began picking wild blackberries off the bushes, dropping them in an old ice cream bucket. By the time we were done, I'd have little trails of dried blood all around my hands from the thorns.

Looking back, I now understand that gathering supper was an event of entertainment and necessity all in one. Once we got home, Maw-maw and I would go into the backyard and line up the fish on plywood. The cicadas and crickets serenaded us while we rubbed spoons up to the fish head in the opposite direction from the scales. When those scales landed on your flesh and dried, they were the hardest to get off. Together, we scaled and gutted in silence. Being near her was enough for me, I felt her love. Water, mud, and fish filled the air. When our work was complete, I savored eating the crisp tail and fins covered in cornmeal with just enough salt and pepper—fresh blackberries covered with mounds of sugar, a rare and cherished feast as dessert. After baths, I would dress for bed with the heat from the sun dancing on my skin.

That is how the fishing trips went when my Maw-maw came with us. Things went a little differently when she stayed home. When Paw-paw took me alone, he filled his red and white ice chest with beer. We would head out to the same fishing spot, but he would turn off in the little town of Delcambre. A fishing town with boats lining the canal that runs through the town. The air smelt of shrimp and water. We would pick up Mr. Dexter. This man seemed older than God and lived in a house that I was positive would collapse at any moment. If you've ever watched the Munsters, he looked like Herman minus the green paint. Mr. Dexter was, for the most part, a very nice but perpetually drunk man. Together, all three of us would fish, with me sitting on a turned-over bucket, always watching for alligators or snakes. Sitting as still as a statue, I would jump occasionally because of a mysterious movement in the cattails. When the afternoon clouds started rolling in, we picked up our gear and returned to drop off Mr. Dexter.

One day Paw-paw pulled into the bar and told me to get out of the car. I was amazed at how dark it was inside; the smell of stale beer and cigarettes made it hard to breathe, but the air was ice cold. He put me down on a barstool between him and Mr. Dexter. I don't remember the face of the bartender; I only know she was a woman, a pretty one. Together they ordered drink after drink while steadily lighting and crushing Marlboro Reds. I watched the red tips of their cigarettes go up and down as I drank cherry Coke after cherry Coke. Eventually, I drifted off.

I was in the car when I woke up, sliding on the red vinyl seats. Paw-paw had a hard time keeping the car between the lines. For whatever reason—maybe we were too late getting back, maybe he needed the bathroom, or maybe he was just that shit-faced; whatever the case, maybe only I could see that the drawbridge lights flashing and about to open, but Paw-paw only sped up. Like the Dukes of Hazzard, we flew over that bridge right before it opened to let a shrimp boat through. I thought Paw-paw and Mr. Dexter would both piss on themselves laughing. We never talked about that ride.

When we got home, the conversation had an entirely different tone. After dropping Mr. Dexter off, we pulled into the driveway. Maw-maw, who was seething, met us in the driveway. She went to the driver's window, cursing in French. Demanding he stay away from that bar. Maw-maw was private enough not to reveal more. Her fits were fast but ferocious. Threatening to end her own life. Seeing that side of her was rare but terrifying.

Laying in bed, I would imagine Maw-maw being gone. My skin would tingle while my heart raced. Eventually, I would jump out of bed, needing to feel my feet on the floor. Otherwise, I was convinced I would drift off into an unknown abyss. Moments like those went quickly.

Saturdays meant Bourré games; they alternated between the houses of friends of my grandparents—a feast of foods like barbeque, boudin, gumbo, stew, and countless desserts. Paw-paw would summon me to grab him a Schlitz from the fridge. On my way to the card table, I would pull the triangular tab back and take a sip off the top. If it were a winning night, he'd put a kitty aside for me with a couple of quarters. The men and women usually sat at separate card tables. The men drank and smoked while the women gossiped and ate. The kids watched TV and stayed out of the way.

Mrs. Robicheaux hosted the Saturday night Bourre. I liked visiting her house because she made the tiniest meatballs with a sweet, spicy sauce. Food like this was an event for me. Although Paw-paw worked, we never had a stocked pantry. During the week, we ate eggs and rice more often than not. We did not have extra money, leading to tension between Maw-maw and Paw-paw. He worked, but it was not enough.

This night was like any other; the men were getting louder and louder while the smoke began crawling across the ceiling. We arrived during the day; now it was pitch black out. My eyes were heavy when I heard a commotion from the women's card table. Everyone began talking loudly. I knew it was bad because I had never seen every adult leave their money on the tables unattended. Everyone crowded around Mrs. Robideaux. Strangers in uniforms rushed through the storm door with what looked like a whiteboard. Then I heard someone say, "Take off her brassiere." One of the men dressed in uniform did just that and put something on her chest that made Mrs. Robideaux flop like a fish. Mrs. Robideaux was dead, and the Boureé game was over.

Chapter 2

For the first seven years of my life, I depended on my grandparents after being left by my mom. I never imagined living with anyone else until one day. I was in the kitchen while the entire house was packed up. Paw-paw stood over me, assisting me in packing my toys, while Maw-maw was packing the rest of the house. I didn't understand the magnitude of what was unfolding as Maw-maw packed up the house when I was seven.

Years later, I understood. Paw-paw had gone bankrupt and, in turn, lost the house. On the other hand, Mom had just given birth to one of my sisters and decided I should move in with her. The timing of my sister's birth and the financial loss to my grandparents relocated me permanently with Mom.

My mind awakened from the fog while lying on a pallet of blankets in the living room of a shotgun-style house. A lamp was on, minus the shade. Mac, my mother's boyfriend, knelt beside me.

"When am I going home?" I don't remember being scared; I'm just homesick.

"You are home."

Mom sat on her bed, smoking a joint. As I lay on the floor beneath the fog of her smoke, I felt a hole of darkness open within my gut. I was falling through, spinning. I stared from where I was on the floor into the doorway of her room with an enormous waterbed with a mustard-yellow sheet and a crib against the wall. My sister was in her crib with sweaty blonde curls framing her face. I rolled over; there was simply nothing to keep me awake.

The house was alien to what I was used to. Maw-maw and Paw-paw's house was brick with a yard. I had a swing set and a room. The air was thick and heavy, even with the windows open. The sound of the cicadas and tires rolling over the gravel woke me up in the middle of the night. My room was the living room. If you entered through the front door, you walked in through the living room (my room) straight into my mother's room. If you kept going, you'd be in the kitchen, with a bathroom to the left.

I was now going to start a new school. My old school wasn't easy to get along with, so I was hopeful things would be different at my new school. On the playground at my old school were seesaws, swing sets, and colossal tractor tires painted in primary colors. I was on the playground when a boy asked me if I wanted to play.

Eager, I ran to the seesaw and hopped on like I was mounting a stallion. There I was, chanting, "Seesaw Mardi Gras, Momma's having a baby." Suddenly, the boy pinned my ankles under the metal seat. The boy laughed as he jolted his seat up as fast as he could, leaving me in tears while my ankles felt wrapped in fire.

In the classroom, our mats were kept in the back of the room. Each day after a nap, we were to carry our mats to our cubby and store them. After a while, I refused to take my mat; there was one particular little boy who always pulled his pants off and chased us all around butt-naked.

Nap time created more problems. Every other kid slept on the vinyl blue and red plastic. But my mat was different; it had a purple cover with tiny yellow flowers. Maw-maw made it, especially for me. I was pretending to sleep on this day when I heard, "Psst." I knew better than to crack my lids open; I squeezed them tighter. "Psst. Hey. Look, I got a surprise for you." When I made the tiniest peek, I saw a boy's round face just inches from mine. His breath was hot. His eyes were glowing white in the dark classroom. I tilted my head up to see where Mrs. Arnold was. The light from the hall held her frame as she talked to the other teacher with her back to us. "Ssshh," I replied to the boy, trying to avoid annoying the teacher.

"Look," he said with urgency. I was curious: what did he have? I followed his glance down his mat to see he had his pants down and was pointing his little penis at me. I rolled over. From that day on, I knew how to avoid all the bad things. Each day, I climbed inside a giant tractor tire and pushed my back into the sides of the tire, embraced in a tar-smelling hug during recess.

Living with Mom rocked my brain. She did not spend most of the morning like Maw-maw did, making me brush my teeth and combing my long, sandy brown hair. Nor did she iron my clothes like Maw-maw did. That first morning before school, I sat at the table and waited, waited, and waited. Eventually, I got dressed. I'd never picked out my clothes before. I picked the brightest shirt I could find and blue jeans. The jeans reached right above my ankle bones. My hair wasn't brushed into the fine silky sheet and pulled tightly into its proper ponytail.

I heard the scraping of a lighter and watched the red dot of her cigarette lift up and down in her bed. She was awake, but I was confused about why she wouldn't get up to see that I was ready for school. Following my gut, I walked out the backdoor to find my way. Something told me not to bother her. Like a magnet, I was drawn to the group of kids on the gravel corner. There was a trailer park down our road, so plenty of kids were waiting for the bus. My heart pounded with the anticipation of making friends. I couldn't wait to have my very own group of friends. As I walked up, waiting for everyone to greet me, the giggles stopped, and I was met head-on with eyeballs rolling up and down my body.

"What's your name?"

"Venus."

"You're Venus the penis, Venus the penis." And that was my first day at Magnolia Street.

Chapter 3

My earliest memories of my sister Crystal are of her standing in her crib with a diaper, which seemed full enough to weigh her down. Clothes were not something we wore a lot of, being that we were in southern Louisiana, where relentless heat and the humidity suffocate—with no air conditioner. It didn't take long for me to naturally fall into taking care of her. Mac, Crystal's father, a truck driver, was rarely around. When he was, he would dote on Crystal. Mom lugged her around on her rail-thin hip.

We didn't do much outside of our house. If it wasn't within walking distance, we didn't go. Mom never learned how to drive; neither did Maw-maw. Mom's mode of transportation was a brown bicycle with a wire basket in front. Her long brown, silky hair trailed behind her when she rode her bike away from our house—often leaving me to care for my baby sister. I'd walk her up and down our gravel road.

I learned how to pick out trustworthy friends. If they were rich, they would be mean to us—pretending to want to play, but quickly trying to make fun of our mismatched clothes, or even worse, our house—and if kids wanted to send me strolling away with my head down and pulling Crystal by the arm, they'd make fun of our mom for being a drug dealer.

Once I came home from school and talked about how I was

being taught to "Just Say No," Mom sat me down at her black wooden table, which had a shiny finish that always looked wet. She warned me not to talk to anyone at school about what she smoked as she pulled a hit of a joint. The joint was stuck on the end of an orange flat stone with a green marijuana leaf painted on top. She puckered her lips around the hole on the opposite side of the lit joint. The joint glowed red in front of me. Like a magician, she would turn the entire stone around into her mouth, the lit part and all, exposing the hole to me. I would pucker my lips up just as she would around the hole while she blew the smoke to me. Suddenly, I became heavy with sleep.

When Mac was in from a run, he would drive us around in his big eighteen-wheeler to visit their friends. This always started as a grand adventure but usually ended with some kid I barely knew getting his ass beat, pants down, ass busted up with kitchen utensils or belts. It just came with the territory. It usually boiled down to adults getting drunk or high on whatever drug was around and the kids not wanting to leave them alone, bugging them too much. Crystal and I somehow knew to stay out of the way and enjoy being out of the house. We stayed out of sight, watching the night unfold, until we fell asleep and were carried off.

Mac brought home a friend one night. I didn't pay much attention to any of it. I do faintly remember all three adults sitting around that shiny table. More than anything, I remember how yellow the kitchen was. You could see your reflection on the walls from the glossy paint.

My closet was what should have been the grocery pantry in the kitchen. Mom, Mac, and the new guy all sat around getting high. Mac had his usual beer, but the new guy had a big bottle of brown liquid. Mom was never a drinker. Coca-Cola was her drink of choice. Crystal had Coke in her bottle regularly. I used to love tipping it and watching the stream of Coke shoot out across the room or tilting my head back with her bottle aimed at my mouth while it shot down my throat.

My grandparents took the two of us to spend a weekend with

them. I was so excited. I remember the look on Maw-maw's face when she saw me. She was mortified that my mother had cut off all my hair. It sat clean above my shoulders. I remember standing in the doorway with Crystal propped on my hip. I was no longer the seven-year-old they had dropped off months earlier. I changed.

That weekend, I lay on the floor at night on the side of my grandparents' bed on a pile of blankets while the bedside lamp shone above me. Little did I know how things would change even more when I was brought back to Mom's. When my grandparents brought me back, I wrapped around Paw-paw's leg, screamed, and cried as tears dripped from my chin.

Once I calmed down, I heard Mom on the phone. Mom never used a filter when she spoke. She had no concept of inappropriate words for a child to listen to. When using the bathroom, we didn't tee-tee or poop, or any of those kiddy-type words. And so the conversation unraveled: "I can't fucking believe that gun wasn't loaded. Girl, I had no idea he was coming in. We were both naked in the bed. Mac walked right up and told him to get the fuck up. I kept screaming, 'Don't, Mac, stop!' When Mac put that gun between his eyes, I knew he was gonna kill him. When he pulled the trigger, I couldn't fuckin' believe he didn't blow his brains out."

I sat on the edge of my sofa bed, trying to assemble the pieces of that conversation. Who had Mac tried to shoot? Later that night, I sat in a scalding hot water tub. To do this in a house with no air conditioner would be torture for most people, but to me, it was an escape. Every time I stood up, I had to grab a hold of the side of the tub while my vision went black.

Later that night, I lay in my bed when the door to our house opened. Glenn, the new guy with the big bottle of brown liquid, walked in, and within minutes, I heard the waves of the water bed sloshing around with grunts and groans. No door separated the living room, where I slept, from my mom's room. I learned to squeeze my pillow on my head and close my eyes tight while an ocean-like noise filled my head. On that hot night, I figured out who Mac had pulled the gun on and who had been naked in bed with my mom. I also knew Mac wouldn't be coming home anymore.

There were two things I learned very fast about Glenn. He was young, although I had no idea what this meant since I was only about eight. It was a big deal; he was only eighteen. My mom was in her thirties. The other thing momma ranted about to no end was the fact that his mom was rich. Neither of these things were important to me. At the time, I did notice that he simply paid my sister and me no attention. Not that anyone ever really did. But one thing people always did when they stopped in to buy a bag of weed or smoke a joint was compliment my mom on how pretty or smart we were. But to him, we were just nonexistent. One night, though, that all changed.

Selling weed was what my mom did for a living back then. She had a process and a code of honor that went along with it. She would break her product down into more affordable quantities when she got it. Most girls help bake with their mothers; I got to help her break up the weed. I sat at the shiny table with a silver bowl large enough to bathe a baby in. I would break apart the big chunks, leaving my hands sticky and smelling like a mix of Christmas tree and skunk. I would nibble on the seeds like sunflower seeds.

Dutifully, I would make a stack of large stems and a pile of seeds. Whatever the reason, she had gotten a large block of dry ice on that particular night. Glenn sat across from me with the scale weighing things out. My mom was somewhere. He began to carve little circles into the dry ice block, filling the little circles with Jim Beam. When the drops of Jim Beam froze solid, he popped them out with the tip of a knife. He held one up for me to take. I took the offer.

Mom had a tight circle of friends. In her lifestyle, you don't sell to strangers or bring strangers over—end of discussion. If you planned on leaving with your purchase, you always smoked with her before you left. She'd say that a nark would never actually use drugs. I have no idea if this holds any truth or if it was all just Mom's narrative of things she wanted to believe.

One couple my mom was tight with had no kids: Cindy and

Aaron. The wife was pretty, and the husband was enormous and handsome. I loved how he would throw me high so that the bottom of my stomach felt like it would fall out as he caught me in his bearlike paws. We laughed a lot at their house. These were the only adults who played with my sister and me. Aaron was like a giant, at least in the eyes of a child. They adored Crystal and I, a thirty-something couple with no children who desperately wanted their own.

We would run full speed along the wooden floors. Like most houses in Louisiana, it was built high so my sister and I could walk under it. There is something about a wooden house off the ground with a porch nearly as large as the house itself that opens many possibilities for adventure when you are little.

We were all over at their house one weekend—my mom, Glenn, Crystal, and me. All four adults puckered up to joint after joint. Everyone had a drink in hand except Mom; she had her red can of Coke. She was beautiful, pushing her long brown hair behind her ears while tilting her head back to take a hit. After inhaling, she'd quickly tuck her chin in to hold the choke of the smoke. Her skin at that time was perfect; like most women from the South, her skin was golden. Her body was fluid, thin, and long; she was a natural beauty. She never wore makeup, not even lip gloss. In my mind, my mother was a goddess at this time in our lives.

That night, the adults had a good buzz—the fog of smoke was heavy, and the role of the Yahtzee dice kept going. Crystal and I were lying on their couch; she was sound asleep, pulling on her pacifier in a dream. I was pretending to be dead to the world, which I must have been good at because adults never caught on, and I did this regularly.

The conversation started with, "Let them stay. Come and get them in the morning." I was so excited; my heart was pounding in my chest. We would be princesses for the day. Cindy and Aaron would take us around town or buy us something. I craved attention, and it took everything I had not to squeal in delight and blow my cover.

Aaron offered to carry my sister and me to bed so all four could continue partying in the kitchen. Gently, he placed his log-like arms under my body. I let my head fall off to the opposite side so he wouldn't realize I was playing possum. He strolled into the dark room. The air from the window unit blowing directly towards the bed was ice cold. It was much easier to breathe; once we crossed the doorway, the smoke seemed to stop following us. I was wide awake but tired and ready to fall asleep finally.

He laid me down on my back, my head swallowed by the cold pillow. He was pulling his arm out from under me when he guided his hand down the middle of my back. I could hear Mom and everyone else laughing and coughing in the kitchen. As his arm slid, I realized what path he was taking. His hand stopped right between my legs. My body became hot. I thought my skin would blister. A knot formed in my throat as his hand sat for what seemed like an eternity between my legs, right on top of my satin panties with the little pink bow in the front. I realized I couldn't trust Aaron. I pretended to roll over in my sleep, which startled him; he pulled his hand out and rejoined the party.

The following day, instead of being excited to wake up to the smell of bacon, I tried to make myself stay in bed. I didn't like being in that house anymore and didn't want my sister there. Cindy and Aaron's house had fallen off my list of favorite places. Eventually, I had to get up to use the bathroom. I walked into the living room and saw the giant lying on the couch in a pair of blue jeans cutoff shorts. He snatched me up as I walked past him, plopped me on his belly, and tickled my rib cage. I laughed so hard I snorted.

"Where's Aunt Cindy?" I gasped between snorts.

"She took your sister to the store." Aaron had his teeth clenched into a sort of smile.

In the background, I could hear the wrestling announcer introducing the next match. I wriggled around, forgetting about what he had done the night before. That is until he pushed me down a little farther, and I felt something enormous between my legs. My laughing stopped immediately. I looked straight into his big black eyes. He now had my toothpick arms in his gargantuan

17

grip. He slowly began rocking me back and forth.

"No," I said, shaking my head. No. STOP!" I tried to get down, but it was useless; he had me gripped tightly.

He tilted his head to the side like a puppy and said, "Stop what? I'm just tickling you." He slowly started to rock me again over his erection.

"Stop it! I know what you are trying to do. Let me go." I don't know if I scared him, I don't know if he felt bad, I don't know what the hell it was, but he let me go. At that moment, I realized a lot of things. The first was if I had ever doubted it, there was no adult I could trust. If there were, how come my mom left me there in the first place? Why did my grandparents let me go live with Mom? And how come Aaron had to be a nasty adult? I had to protect my sister from these people and stop being stupid.

Chapter 4

I became vigilant in the role of mothering my sister. I fixed her bottles and changed her diapers without ever being told. With her lying on my chest with her baby-fat thighs hanging over my sides, I would hum her to sleep. Things stayed the same for several months until I realized my mom's belly looked like a small volleyball. This made sense because, when Glenn got home from delivering pizzas, he would make my sister and I stand next to the bed and interrogate us about who had left the Jell-O Pudding Pops wrappers in the yard. I always took the blame. It was right around this time that he started spanking Crystal. Glenn never touched me. Maybe he took his frustrations out on Crystal because her dad tried to shoot his brains out.

My birth parents had been separated for as long as I could remember. Being my dad's only child, I had his full attention when I visited. Unlike my mother, he treated me like a child. The problem was he had his issues, but he tried to protect me from them. Once I moved in with Mom after living with my grandparents, he started taking me for a couple of weeks during the summer. Our visits were filled with amusement parks and parties. I'd barrel down water slides while he stood in his blue jean cutoff shorts, missing was his black Harley Davidson T-shirt. He'd nervously wait for me to bob up in the wading pool. Seeing him standing at the bottom waiting for me with his milky legs he always seemed so nervous. His size overshadowed most people around him. Those summer days, he was my protector anxiously waiting to scoop me up and bring me to the next water slide.

Long motorcycle rides in the Texas heat were some of my favorite memories with him. He would sit braiding my long hair to make sure it didn't tangle in the wind. I was careful with the details I revealed to him about my mom and Glenn. At the time, he did not know how to control his anger other than to deal with it physically. It was nothing for him to challenge a guy to fight if he made the mistake of staring at me or my first stepmom, Dana, for too long.

Weekends at Dad's usually consisted of parties. For what seemed like miles, you could see Harley after Harley parked in a row, leading to the trailer or house that was hosting. Shiny black motorcycles all lean in the same direction, like a line of dominos tempting a slight push. The men mostly looked the same—gray hair, beards to their chest, blue jeans, black Harley T-shirts, and leather vests. Kids ran around popping firecrackers or rolling down dirt hills. It never failed somebody would do something to piss off one of the men, and they'd start banging. I knew to act like I didn't see the commotion. I'd run out of sight with the other kids. Not out of fear for my safety, but to let the grown-ups do what they needed to do, and more than likely wouldn't remember the following day. More often than not, my stepmom or aunt would escort me to the car. I always felt terrible for the other kids there because once the adults got worked up, some kids would get knocked around like aggravating puppies, mainly because they weren't out of sight. Those biker fights weren't meant to be violent. Everyone went back to being brothers the next day. It was how things went in the dark and dusty Texas night.

When I returned to Mom's after my summer break with Dad, protecting Crystal was my purpose, and it shattered me to see her being hurt. I'd wait on the edge of the bed for her to shuffle to me, crying with her pacifier gripped between her teeth and her blonde ringlets clinging to her face, wet from sweat. Soon, mom was expecting another baby. Glenn was cooking more. Growing up, we usually ate on our beds in separate rooms. I can't explain why; our beds were where we spent most of our day watching TV.

I hated eating. Maybe it was the heat or stress. Glenn started trying to get us to sit at the table occasionally. This made our desire not to eat even stronger. Crystal would usually fall asleep at the kitchen table. Her blonde curls swayed back and forth as her head jerked from side to side, both of us sweaty from the heat in the kitchen. Not only did we not have an air conditioner, but we had an old gas stove that always had pilot lights lit. Together, we'd sit for what seemed like hours, staring at our plates of food. Eventually, I got smart, or so I thought, and made a plan to free us. I would scoop most of the contents of our plates into a napkin. I'd shove the mushy mess into my shirt and dump it over the neighbor's fence. To my pleasure, this worked until the teenage boys next door started shouting at me for tossing our food on their basketball court.

Not long after, I noticed quarreling between my mom and Glenn. Eventually, she started screaming about his mom being a bitch, and no one was going to take her children from her. She'd often shout in his face that he was just a momma's boy. He never yelled back or acted like any of this bothered him. It was weird. Instead, though, we seemed to agitate him more and more. He began to take his frustrations out on Crystal more, while Mom began to take her anger out on me verbally. She started screaming that I was a whore or bitch.

School was always challenging for me. I felt like I was sitting under a microscope, alien to my classmates and teachers. I usually sat in the back and prayed never to be noticed. Homework was not something I did; focusing at home wouldn't happen. In addition to taking care of Crystal, I was in charge of most of the chores. One day, I brought a book home to complete an assignment. I always intended to do my work but never got to it. I left the mammoth book on the table. The following day, when I woke, it was gone. I searched high and low. I walked through my mom and Glenn's room and asked if they had seen it. Only to hear, "You shouldn't leave your shit lying around." I was frantic as I remembered the large teacher standing in front of the class and giving a sermon on how expensive these books were, and we were to be very careful with them, or we would be sent to the principal's office and have to pay for them.

We lived in a one-bedroom house with four people crammed into it. There was no place to lose things. I was in a panic; no way did I want to get sent to the principal's office. I could feel the bile in my stomach churning as I stepped off the bus. I was terrified of being fussed at for losing the book. I was feeling a full-fledged panic attack. I spotted a book sack against the brick wall where we were all supposed to line up our sacks while on the playground. Quickly, I snatched it up and ran around the corner. I frantically scratched out the other kid's name and scribbled in mine. It never dawned on me that my teacher would know it was not her handwriting, much less a child's. Thankfully, she never said anything to me; she acted like everything was normal. Weeks later, I came across my reading book in Glenn's things. Lesson learned: I never attempted to bring home another textbook again.

Soon, Mom started going on tangents like never before about Glenn and his mother, who seemed like a big mystery to me. After all, she had never stepped foot in our house up to this point. I only remember seeing her white Cadillac parked outside our house while Glenn walked up to the driver's side window and took cash from her. She was old; that was all I could see. Eventually, mom started screaming into the telephone receiver that this woman would never take her kids and *fuck her* for threatening to call the police. The intensity of Mom's anger and paranoia escalated quickly. Mom was never the average mom before, but her anger became rage. Just like Glenn, we seemed to agitate her more, resulting in daily screaming fits referring to us as bitches, whores and sluts. Eventually, I looked up the words in the dictionary. Wanting to know what the difference was between the profanities.

One afternoon, with the air hot and heavy, I strolled off my school bus, walked up the steps to the front porch, and opened the front door to my bedroom. The entire house was empty. The only things present were bits of trash here and there. I stood terrified;

where was Crystal? Alone in a gutted house, I had nothing to do but panic. It was a dreadful feeling of standing perfectly still but, oddly enough, being sucked down into a black hole of nothingness. It was a feeling I was experiencing more frequently.

In the corner of my closet lay a black velvet marker poster of a unicorn I had started to color and never finished. It was torn on the floor. It could have been being left behind in an empty house, possibly being left behind as a toddler, or could it have been being taken back as a child? In any case, I was standing scared and alone, and I started to shake. I stood and trembled in a darkness that gobbled me up. Eventually, I heard tires crunching over the gravel outside. They had come back for me.

Chapter 5

I remember neither arriving nor setting foot in our new home for the first time. My mind flashes to a scene of living in rural Abbeville, Louisiana. At the time, there wasn't much to see in Abbeville, especially since mom didn't drive. I don't remember getting out much, except to go to school. I grew excited when I realized I lived in the same town as my grandparents; it was only about a ten-minute walk along a highway to their house. Most of the time, Paw-paw would rescue me from our new shotgun house, taking me for sleepovers at their home. It was explained to me that we had to leave New Iberia because Mom was convinced Glenn's mother was trying to have all of us taken away. She was also certain Glenn's mom was trying to get her arrested. That's when she decided to pack us up and relocate without telling Glenn or most of their friends. The problem was that the mom was about to give birth to her third baby, who happened to be Glenn's child. It still amazes me how people adapt to situations. Here was my mother, who didn't work and never drove, but she still could relocate us within hours.

One thing I vividly remember about Abbeville was the chickens that lived on the other side of the fence. I used to sit on the porch and pretend they were my pets, throwing food scraps through the chain link fence. This move also meant that I had to attend another new school. I was visibly poor now; I wore pants that were too short for my long legs and had tangled hair.

I was not nearly as bright as the other kids were. Compared to my peers, who created beautiful art projects and worked on the longest math word problems I typically skipped, I was beyond an outcast; I realized I wasn't as smart as them. This caused a whole new set of insecurities. Reading aloud in class was torture to me. I couldn't pronounce the words most of my classmates did with ease. I remember being asked what planet I lived on, and I had no idea. I sat with my head down until the teacher got tired of waiting for me to answer questions and simply stopped calling on me.

In the new place, there is calmness in our house. Mom no longer screamed since Glenn wasn't around. I don't remember much other than Crystal staying in the front room with me. Once again, our room was supposed to be the living room, and there was a large kitchen next to my mom's room. Now, there was a new baby in the crib, Rose. Memories of baby Rose escapes me. My mind blacked out the memories of her crawling, crying, or learning to talk. One minute, Rose was in a crib; the next, she was a young adolescent. I remember rambling uncontrollably to my mother about how happy I was when it was just us, and she replied that this was how it would be. Don't get me wrong, Mom wasn't waking up and tending to my sister and me, nor was she concerned with us much. She wasn't interested in winning any mother-of-the-year-award, but the calmness was enough for me. For the most part, Crystal and I kept to ourselves, wandering up and down the gravel road and highway.

This was also when I began loving music. I often listened to the radio on that front porch and learned the words to almost every song. If I was in the kitchen, I carried the boombox with me. When I'd bathe, it sat next to the tub. Music took me far away, and music always knew my mood. At night, when I became lonely, music comforted me to sleep.

Like a slide in a movie projector waiting to be pulled, my mind flips to my most vivid memory of Abbeville. I was sick from school, lying on the bottom bunk, when mom knelt beside me. For a second, I thought she was coming to touch my forehead to see if I needed anything like the moms on the Tylenol commercials.

Instead, she pushed her hair behind her ear and spoke the words I couldn't believe, "Glenn's coming over tonight." The fast-forward button gets pressed on my boombox, and they are married. I am now ten years old.

Chapter 6

We move again, this time back to New Iberia on a dead end road. If you drove past our house and continued on about four or five more houses, you would drive right into the muddy Bayou Teche. This move was different. I was older and felt like more of an outcast. This was my fifth-grade year. What I hated the most about our house wasn't the cracked white paint but the rusted screened-in porch. We had a living room inside, but we did not use it. Most families sat and watched TV in their living rooms, not ours; you just walked through ours. The house had two bedrooms. I had the second bedroom while Crystal and Rose shared a utility room as their bedroom. The TV was in Mom and Glenn's room. There, all three of us would sit on the floor at the foot of my mom's bed, watching the screen with the faint sound of her roach clip ringing on the glass ashtray as a tail of smoke crawled up to the ceiling.

Here is where the anger came out in us, like a flow of heat radiating through the open windows. Gone was our calm; the wave of screaming matches was due to many things. Our house was sandwiched between Glenn's friends. They were all his age; therefore, they all liked to hang out in the yard, drinking and getting high on whatever they had. My mom became increasingly reclusive and did not want Glenn hanging out in the yard. The downside was that my sisters and I felt Glenn's and Mom's wrath. Glenn took out his frustrations mostly on Crystal, while Mom targeted me. It was not unusual to see me flying through the screen door, resembling a victim running from a raging fire, my brown hair tangled in my mom's hand yanking me back. She started striking me with flailing blows that I quickly learned to return, which mostly limited her hitting. She still screamed at the top of her lungs until the veins stuck out on her skin. Eventually, the hitting between Mom and I ceased, but the violent words never.

We were the circus on our street. This was when I started stealing my mom's weed and smoking it with the boys down by the bayou. Eventually, I met a girl who lived in the last house before the road ran directly into the bayou. Her name was Heaven; she had blonde cotton-candy-like hair; she became my friend. Her mom was a thick woman with the same soft, poofy blonde hair as her daughter. I walked the couple of houses down to hers. When I opened the door, her mom was belting out Tina Turner with a glass in her hand, ice cubes clinking along the wall of the glass. She twirled around, laughing and singing. Heaven didn't pay much attention to her mother's stage skills. A man walked out from the dark hallway. My only memory of him was that he was nice, although I never heard him speak. The next time I went over, Heaven's mom wasn't laughing and singing any longer but was passed out on the couch spread eagle with the same sweaty glass next to her. That was the last appearance of the quiet man in the dark hallway but the first of many times I spent at Heaven's. Usually, her mom was passed out or looked like a zombie. She spoke with a British accent and let us have the most kick-ass gatherings any ten-year-old could think of. The booze came from her, and the weed from my house.

One night, a handful of us stood at the end of the gravel road in front of Heaven's. We passed a roach around. Her mom was inside with a boy our age, teaching him God knows what. We just stood in silence until Heaven decided to go on inside. As drunk as her mom was, she always wanted our company; this was foreign to me. At home, my mother locked herself away. When I was home, I retreated to the safety and calmness of my room. The living room always remained empty, and there was no television to coax us into sitting together. Despite Heaven's mom drinking, she cared for Heaven when she was awake. She purchased her clothes that fit and did the usual mom stuff with her.

I started having my period around this time. Maybe it was my age, lack of eating properly, or the suffocating heat in our house, but when my time hit, the bleeding simply would not stop, and I soaked through pad after pad. My mom thought I was using them for other reasons, and once my supply was gone, that was it. She locked up hers, and I had to beg Heaven to help me. Wadding up cheap toilet paper in my underwear only lasted a few minutes before it became a disaster. Heaven's mom simply could not fathom me not having sanitary items, and she supplemented my supply as needed for a short time.

It wasn't long before the day came when I walked down to Heaven's house, and they were gone. All that was left were trash and empty vodka bottles. Years later, in my early twenties, I ran into one of the boys from our street. He marveled over what he had learned from our parties at Heaven's house. Funny, the things people remember.

Chapter 7

During this time, my mother became more hateful towards us. Also, my fourth and final sibling, David, came along. At this point, I just remember him popping up one day. Truthfully, I don't remember much about him being a baby. I was much more adult-like than any other kid my age. One afternoon, I got off the bus and walked into my bedroom to find every item of clothing thrown on the floor. Every dresser drawer emptied the contents on my floor. Notes that were once folded lay open as evidence someone had read them. I stood and trembled with anger. I had nothing and was well aware of this, but every item I did have was tossed about like trash. Now, I was left to clean it all up. No reason was given other than that I hadn't completed some random chore to Glenn's liking. Slowly, I began to pick things up, and I screamed at the blank walls with no reply.

One day, while I was sitting in class, possibly fifth grade, two women stood at the door with what looked like chopsticks. Stillness filled the room as if you could hear every kid choking back saliva over sandpaper-lined throats. I felt like I was being dangled from a string.

One by one, we tilted our heads; the women rolled their splintery sticks through our hair strands. I sat silent, perfectly still, convinced my heartbeat could be heard by the kid next to me. I could hear my blood swooshing through my veins. When she gently tilted my head forward, the stick played on my scalp, sending tiny goose bumps down my arms and the back of my neck. Too quickly, she broke her sticks in two and tapped my shoulder. At first, I pretended not to notice, then realized every kid had turned to face me. She continued to tap my shoulder and pointed to the door. As I stood and walked, every kid stared. As adults, we understand lice are a nuisance and say nothing about the cleanliness of a person, nor does having them mean that a person has germs or some debilitating disease. But as adults, we also know how cruel kids can be; they are ruthless.

As I stood across the counter in the office, the secretary dialed my house. Gripping the counter, I was no longer concerned with the room full of kids teasing me; anxiety had the hairs covering my body standing at attention. I knew what was going to happen even before I heard Mom's shrill voice through the telephone. It was so loud that the secretary held the phone away from her ears.

"That fucking little bitch! I don't drive. What do you want me to do?" Complete and total humiliation blanketed my soul. My mother called us all fucking little bitches regularly. I was used to it. The thought of someone else knowing that she called me this was crippling to me. The secretary, now visibly annoyed, sent me to another room. A short time later, I looked up to see a strange black man I'd never seen in my life looking down at me. I knew he was there for me, but I honestly had no clue who he was.

"Who are you?" I asked.

"The cab driver," he replied without a bit of expression. *Fuck*, that is all I thought. There was absolutely nothing I could do. Not only did I have lice, but my mother spewed profanities to the school secretary, who probably couldn't wait to blab about it to every teacher in the school. And now, every kid who already had something cruel to say about me would see me walking out with some random man, and they would also see me getting into a dirty yellow cab. They'd know my mom simply did not give a shit. Walking out under the giant oak trees was like stepping in a parade with every classroom window focused on me.

When he pulled up to the sidewalk, I could see her

through the rusted screen door, a slim shadow with flowing hair. Before she spoke, she was stunning, her skin the perfect tan, slender and natural. Then her mouth opened, the door moaned as it flung open, and it snapped shut, wood on wood, sending a cracking noise into the street. Mom marched to the cab with her sandy hair flowing behind her. I started towards the door, but she grabbed me before I could make it through the door frame.

"You're not going in my fucking house. Take off your clothes. They are everywhere on you, little bitch." When she screamed, really screamed, she foamed at the mouth. I stood looking at her— inside, I pleaded for her to grab me and tell me it was all OK. I wish she would have told me not to worry about what the other kids thought, that it was perfectly normal and happened all the time. She didn't, and I knew she never would. I stood on the sidewalk and peeled my clothes off, down to my underwear. The neighbors watched as usual. Inside, the skunk smell mixed with incense filled the thick, hot air. Behind me she trailed closely, ordering me to the tub. I began to sob from the intensity of the day, from her screaming at me, the embarrassment of having lice. I stepped into the scalding hot bath as she poured bleach into the water.

That evening I sat on the front porch swing, as Glenn calmly and gently pulled every strand of my brown hair through his fingernails to remove the nits. He had shot squirrels from the front porch and had them cooking on the stove. The stress of the day, the anger I felt, and the lack of air from not having an air conditioner, made me sick to my stomach. The smell of the squirrels cooking was tempting me to vomit. I got sent home two other times with head lice. The last time I promised God that if he would make the lice go away, I'd never eat ice cream again forever. I never got sent home again, but I still ate ice cream.

There was simply no way to predict my mother's moods. She could quickly go from cursing me and anyone else out to laughing and singing at the top of her lungs. Music continuously flowed through the rooms in our home, usually classic rock. I knew every song on the radio. With our windows always open, the neighbors got a show from either my mom or me every day. We'd belt out tunes from the bottom of our hearts. Music was an escape. Sandy was a good friend of my mom's and a loyal customer. She stopped in to buy her usual bag of weed. One day, I was walking along the side of our house to the laundry shed in the back with a basket of laundry on my hip.

"V," Mom shouted from the front porch. She was high, I could tell.

"V, get dressed. You're going to a concert."

"What?"

"Sandy wants me to front her a bag. She's got an extra ticket. You can

go."

I screamed and ran into the house. There was no way to predict my mother's mood, and I didn't dwell on questions when the situation was favorable. I enjoyed those moments because I knew I would be back to reality once they were over.

Glenn and his friends often hung out in their garage. My mother would scream from the back door for him to get into the house—like a mother yells for her children to get inside after dark. Usually, he started by ignoring her. The guys would just stand around some carcass of metal they had been taking apart while they smoked cigarettes, drank, and did whatever other drug Glenn was hiding from Mom. Mom could have easily joined them; no one ever tried to exclude her. Despite Glenn's plea to come out, she'd stay locked in her bedroom, watching television day and night. I felt sorry for him because of the way she'd yell at him to get in the house. It wasn't like she needed him for anything; she just wanted him watching TV in the room with her. Some days, he obeyed and came inside with his bare feet dragging on the wooden floors. Other times, he'd defy her, which only escalated her screaming obscenities out the door for the neighbors to hear. The neighbors looked at me like I was a hurt animal. They never actually asked why my mother acted the way she did; they just whispered and stared like I could fall apart at any moment.

Chapter 8

Not long after this, Glenn's mother wanted him to return to college. Despite being barely in his twenties, she found us a rental house in Lafayette, so we had to move again. She would pull up outside in her white Cadillac, and Glenn would lean in to talk to her through the open window until she provided an envelope with money. She rarely came inside but agreed to pay most of our living expenses if Glenn finished his nursing degree. She was a wealthy, stern woman with a strained relationship with my mother. Despite their differences, they talked on the phone daily. Unfortunately, Glenn's mother struggled with cancer for most of her life. She disapproved of his chosen lifestyle with my mother but supported us as much as possible. Now and then, she would take me shopping for new school clothes and discuss her disapproval of my mother, expecting me to be different. I often overheard my mother screaming at her on the phone. "I'll dance on your fucking grave!" My mother's screams would vibrate through the walls. I had no idea what would start the fights, but those conversations often ended with her screaming vulgarities and slamming the receiver down. This continued until his mother's death after a very long battle with cancer.

The new house was located within walking distance of the university in a much larger city than any we had lived in before. We were in the heart of town, just two blocks from downtown and across the street from a massive church we never attended. The house was magnificent, with a brick exterior and an enormous porch with brick walls. Glenn's mother had funded the entire move and was paying most of our bills so that he could finish college. The high ceilings made my voice echo off the dull wooden floors as I entered the house. My room even had its own small bathroom, offering a sense of retreat and normalcy. Each room had multiple doors, creating a maze-like layout. We closed off the extra doors with furniture, making it clear that the intention was not to gather together in shared spaces. The living room only had a couch and an armchair. My baby brother's crib was placed in the dining room, and as I walked by, I remember seeing him gnawing on the wood of his crib with a soggy diaper hanging much lower than it should have been.

Behind the house were three tiny efficiency apartments my mom would manage for the landlords, and just beyond them was a graveyard less than two feet away. I could even read the tombstones from my bedroom window. I spent many hours sitting on the tombs, finding solace in the cooler air under the trees and wondering about the children who had died so young, fearing the same fate for myself. A wrought-iron fence separated our yard from the graves, and I often jumped over it to read the headstones. I often wondered how the children had died so young, worried the same thing would happen to me.

Chapter 9

One afternoon, as I was walking into the house, I heard a baby crying. I checked on my little brother to find out he was not in the house. Days later, my younger sisters started crying and refused to go to bed.

"What's wrong? Just go to bed," I told Crystal.

Crystal shook her sweaty blonde waves back and forth. "NO," she cried, gripping my waist tightly with her lanky legs.

"Tell me why not."

"Because that lady in white walks her baby back and forth when it cries. Her husband does, too."

I felt a chill run up my back and down my arms. I realized Crystal was telling me what she had seen. Later, Mom told me that Rose had told her the same story.

There was a presence in the house that I simply cannot explain. Perhaps it was created by my mom's repeated storytelling, which easily influenced us. As the years went on, the stories grew. David played video games and talked over his shoulder as if a friend sat beside him. When asked who he was talking to, he'd point to a space and say "her." At the same time, while doing my makeup at my vanity, I felt the sensation of another person pressing their face next to mine as if comparing our faces in the mirror.

I don't know what was happening in our house, but I know there was nothing I could explain.

My mother, who was never religious, convinced Glenn's mother to send a priest to bless our house. One night, he splashed the entire house with holy water. This ritual made me uneasy. The realization that there was something present, and now we were at the mercy of a priest.

Conversations about this lingering presence of a supernatural force continued to be a part of our lives. The stories grew as my mom narrated them in detail into my adulthood. Years later, she'd rely on a self-proclaimed Shaman to release the demons and help spirits cross over that were haunting her.

Chapter 10

Even before my sister Crystal was born, I believed she was destined to be my responsibility. It was almost as if our bond had developed before we ever really laid eyes on each other. Crystal's father, a truck driver, lived a truck driver's lifestyle. He never settled in one place but traveled from town to town.

At some point, Glenn and my mother attached a burden onto Crystal as the sole bearer of all that was wrong in our household. If Crystal hit Rose, it was not uncommon for our mother to scream, "You evil bitch!" over and over. Crystal was demonized for the simple acts of defiance. She would be summoned to sit in a dark corner for hours when she did something forbidden. Eventually, like most kids, Crystal began fighting back, cursing and screaming at Glenn and our mom. She was only in elementary school, but her eyes reflected years beyond her age. Often, Glenn would hit her in the head for being mean to the younger kids or if she lied when confronted. As the months passed, I became more and more protective of her. I wanted to protect her from being hurt.

During this point, my mother started lashing out, screaming that if she had to choose between Crystal and Glenn, it would be Crystal who would have to go. One day, I walked around the house, and Crystal was gone. Crystal was taken to a psychiatric hospital. Mom and Glenn claimed she was out of control and hurting the other two children. When

Crystal returned home some days later, I noticed she wasn't the same. Whatever spark was present before she went was somehow gone. She had absolutely no emotional expression. I was disgusted when I realized she was being medicated. She wasn't the one who needed medication. Soon, the medication stopped, and our situation continued to escalate. Years later, Crystal shared what that experience was like. In a family group session, the staff at the facility stated to Mom and Glenn; your daughter isn't the problem; you are.

Sitting in my room one hot afternoon, my mom opened my door and asked me to go with her. Considering my mother didn't drive, I knew we'd be walking. She took me to a used bookstore down the block. I had never read a book, had never even considered it. I knew my mom read, but I never paid much attention. When we left, she had an armful of books, including one for me, *Cujo*. That day, my mother gave me the gift of reading. She ignited a love inside of me I didn't know existed. Reading turned into a refuge. I could stay in my room for hours and experience a different world. My mom would give me her novels by Stephen King and V.C. Andrews. Eventually, reading turned into a passion for writing. I'd fill notebook after notebook with poetry and journal entries. Reading and writing kept me safe and at peace.

Not long afterward, wandering downtown, I stepped into a public library. I would sit for hours regularly, randomly searching the computer catalog for poetry. I pulled out book after book. I knew very little about the authors or the meaning behind their poems. There were couches in the middle of the room. I would pretend to be sitting in my living room as I became consumed by the pages of the books. I grew to feel at home in that library.

We didn't have money for me to be in extracurricular activities, but reading became my sport. If I found myself bored or simply too hot sitting in my room, I'd walk down to the library and read. I sat in the mammoth building surrounded by strangers and silence. The sweet smell of old paper filled my chest, relaxing my tense body. Eventually, I started bringing my notebook and writing poetry. I never realized I could check out the books for free. Years later, my mother would take me, and I got my first library card. Literature was becoming my love.

Living in a big city was an adjustment for me. Before, we would flip-flop between New Iberia and Abbeville, small towns where everyone knew everyone else. Not only was Lafayette big, but we were living downtown, surrounded by the college campus. Things were busy; college kids parked along our yard to walk to their classes.

I walked the streets alone to get out of the house. More often than not, I wandered the streets downtown barefoot and aimless. I'd walk to the convenience store a few blocks from home to buy mom cigarettes. One day, as I walked through the parking lot, I saw a man sitting in his car. He was smiling at me, not a usual friend. *How are you doing?* Smile, but a weird, *secret* kind of smile. I stared at him, trying to figure out the inside joke.

My gut always seemed to awaken in a bad situation, the kind where your curiosity can lead you to get killed. As my hair marched to an upright position up and down the back of my neck—despite it being a zillion degrees outside—I turned and started marching down the sidewalk toward my house. I knew something wasn't right. I didn't need to turn around to see the man was following me very slowly in his car. I didn't understand why I was so afraid at that moment, but I was smart enough to know that I should keep walking and stay near the grass and as far away from the passenger door of his car as possible. Finally, he slowed and drove beside me; I noticed the passenger window rolled down. I was desperately trying not to look, but as my head turned to face him, I saw the same despicable grin flashing his square teeth. When I looked down, I was completely frozen for a second.

I could not believe what I was seeing. Looking down, I

saw that he was completely naked and rubbing his penis up and down. I ran so fast it felt like I left my stomach on the sidewalk behind me. Bolting up the front steps and tearing through the screen door, I ran to my mom's room. Plopping down on her waterbed, I sent waves crashing against her wooden headboard, "Mom! This man, he..." I rattled off the story. At that moment, she was mother-of-the-year as she dialed the police to report the pervert.

Chapter 11

Although my grandparents raised me until I was seven, my Paw-paw, who raised me, was not my biological grandfather. My mother's biological father was a small-town pimp when she was a child who had, over the years, mentally deteriorated. In his life, he fathered many illegitimate children. It is not uncommon for adults to reach out with a biological connection. Occasionally, my uncle would bring him over to smoke and visit with my mom. He was thin with long gray hair; he slicked it back with Crisco, using a bread tie for a rubber band. Even as an old man, his home was open to prostitutes and addicts.

Growing up, Maw-maw told me about him deserting her for other women he prostituted while she was left behind to care for their dying infant, my mom and uncle, living in poverty. As I grew older, I would listen to my grandmother relive those earlier years. Her strength and resiliency was inspiring. She described her childhood working in cotton fields, living without water or electricity. As she described her first marriage and hardships, my Paw-paw would chime in on how he met her. Pride filled his words as he went through the details of starting a life and family with her children as his stepchildren. Maw-maw would relive caring for an infant while his biological father was nowhere to be found. Through those stories, she never displayed anger. She never portrayed herself as a victim. She was just sharing her past.

My biological grandfather and uncle were brilliant and, without a doubt, retained more knowledge about things in the world than I could fathom. My biological grandfather would go off on a tangent during a conversation. "See, when the Earth spins, it spins energy with it. We are all a part of this thing, man—you, me, him, and her. We come together and make up this big . . ." At that point, I would get up and walk out. I knew the conversation would no longer be comprehensible. It was like randomly pulling encyclopedias off a shelf, reading a page, pulling another, and reading. Over and over. During this time, my uncle would begin ranting about how women are at fault for the state of the world, all the way back to Eve eating the apple. I heard lectures about how evil women were. Like my mother, he could be the kindest person one minute, then suddenly go down a rabbit hole with a random series of facts.

For a while, one of my mother's many half-sisters came around; she had cotton-white hair, toasted skin, and a perfectly long and lean body. Physically, she was the polar opposite of my mom, wearing short cutoffs and makeup. She'd come over and get high. Somehow, I figured out she was a prostitute. Yet I was allowed to go to her trailer to hang out. She'd dance and sing in the kitchen. One day, her little boy, who was about the same age as me, upset her. As she beat him, I knew to sit at the kitchen counter and pretend not to see a thing. That was the last time I went to her trailer. Randomly, she would appear with different men from time to time while I was growing up. Sometimes, she'd have black eyes that she never had to explain. Mom eventually stopped communicating with her.

Around this time, I began hearing the words crack cocaine through these distant and close relatives. At that time, I didn't understand the debilitating addiction this drug caused. As an adult, I now realize how many of the adults in my life were involved with this drug. Slowly, the dots connected to mental illness and paranoia add in crack cocaine; it doesn't leave much hope.

Years later, sitting in a psychology course on addiction, I was astounded by the chemical process that occurs in the human brain during drug use, especially cocaine. There, in that college classroom, I felt like everything made sense. Surrounded by so much chaos growing up, I couldn't help but feel I had dumb luck.

Chapter 12

With the new house came new connections for my mother and new drugs for my stepfather. It wasn't long before their fighting got more heated. I was now in middle school. Aunt Cara, who was about eighteen, started taking me to clubs. She and her friends would buy me a daiquiri to start the Saturday night off. She'd dress me up like a raunchy Barbie. We'd hit the road, fully loaded with half a ton of Maybelline and Aqua Net. Usually, by the time we arrived, I was stumbling over myself, barely able to walk straight. I danced in strobe lights until I became dizzy.

I often drew the attention of much older guys who'd try and pick me up. Aunt Cara's best friend Keith would laugh at them when he revealed I was only eleven. This went on for as long as I can remember. Keith watched over me closely. When the alcohol would finally get to me, he would find me retching in the dark. He'd walk me back to his car, unlock it, lay me on the back seat, and lock the door. Checking on me several times during the night. Now I understand how important it was that he did this, and I am thankful someone was looking out for me.

Eventually, I started building a reputation. I would bring alcohol, pills, and weed to school. Although we lived in a new town, things were the same regarding my mother's constant screaming. We were accustomed to being called bitches and whores. Things had changed with Glenn; he became brutal with

Crystal. I learned not to back down; I could scream just as loudly. Glenn began shooting up. He simply didn't have the strength to battle with me. It was easier for him to knock the shit out of my younger sister. He would sit her in the dark hall on a wooden chair for hours: "You can get up when you start seeing a circle on the wall." She'd sit there and stare with sweat dripping down her face. Or she would do something like leave trash on the floor, and he would walk up behind her with his graduation ring turned around. He slapped her on her head, leaving a knot as a reminder under her tangled hair.

We existed in rage. The stress from the hollering and crying made me frantic. I'd run out of the house without shoes and roam the streets for hours. One night, I was lying on my mom's waterbed, listening to the clicking of the ceiling fan; I heard her on the phone. She hadn't been able to get any weed in weeks, which meant there was none to sell, so she wasn't making extra money. More importantly, her stash was running out. Suddenly, I realized a girl who usually bought small amounts from her offered to get my mom a couple of pounds. I knew something wasn't right.

My mom came into her room excited and opened her cedar armoire to get out the cash.

"Mom, don't you think it's weird that you are her dealer and you can't get any, but she can?"

"It's cool, it's cool." She started hollering for Glenn to drive her to meet this woman.

I turned on MTV and began watching the music awards. Several hours later, while I talked on the phone—the kids were all asleep—I heard her best friend's voice calling my name frantically from the front of the house: "Venus, Venus!" I knew before anyone told me my mom was busted. "Where's her stash? They're coming for you and the kids; hurry, we gotta go, the cops are coming. Clean everything out."

I jumped up, opened the armoire, and began removing whatever I needed to. I don't remember who grabbed who, but we were all in her car within minutes. She drove us to my grandparents, and there we stood. There was no explanation; we simply went inside. The stay didn't last long; eventually, someone came and got us and took us back home.

The story I was told was something like this. When my mom and Glenn pulled up at the truck stop, Mom got out, exchanged the money for the pounds of weed, and was surrounded by cops with guns. Glenn claimed he didn't know Mom was there to buy weed. Mom later told me she was OK with that because he was in school and didn't want him to lose everything he'd worked for. Mom took the wrap and did the time. What Mom didn't understand was the magnitude of her choice to save her husband and neglect us.

Chapter 13

Mom had to report to serve her ninety-day sentence during our summer break from school. I was walking near the university when Glenn slowed down while driving Mom to jail. She had her hair parted down the middle with braids on each side. She stuck her head out the car window and screamed, making funny faces and laughing, childlike. My friend walking with me thought it was funny. I knew what I witnessed was not normal, and it wouldn't get better soon. My mom was going to jail, and we were left with Glenn, his addiction, and good intentions.

It didn't take long to figure out what would happen that summer. After a few days, Glenn didn't bother coming home, leaving me, a thirteen-year-old with three kids. We had a large freezer, and I would defrost whatever we needed to cook. Together, we'd hang out on the front porch like a stage to the world. Next door was a house with two college guys who kept an eye out for us but otherwise minded their own business. We used the church parking lot as a playground when the sun went down. Running through the outside staircases, I played hide-and-seek with the kids. It wasn't long before we caught the attention of another house where several older guys lived, and they joined the party. One of the guys had long, curly blonde hair, and I knew he was much too old to be hanging around a middle-school girl.

Unfortunately, I went over one night after the kids fell asleep, and I'd had too much Everclear to drink. I was the only girl there, with several grown men around. Laughter, smoke, and booze filled the air. I was wearing cutoffs and a white T-shirt. By all means, I was more intelligent than what I showed to be that night. I wanted attention. I was bored. When the thirty-something biker asked me if I wanted to go inside, I knew it wasn't to look at his records, but I still went. It started with kissing. When he closed his door, I knew I had crossed the line. This wasn't going to be easy. Maybe he started kissing me too hard; I don't remember what set me off. I panicked. I wanted out. I could have just laid there and gotten it over with, but I refused.

I shot up. "Get off of me!" Trying to wiggle free, I think I caught him off guard. He didn't hear me. "Get the fuck off of me." At first, he tried to be gentle to relax me, but I started hitting him and screaming, "I said, get the fuck off of me!" I could hear the laughter and rock music outside.

I stood in the corner, using my hands as shields to block everything from candles to glasses being hurled at me. At that moment, I didn't give a shit what he hit me with. Deep inside, I knew I was better than letting this guy get the best of me, a middle-school girl. I don't know why, but he opened the door, and I walked out. I walked past his group of friends and through the vacant lot to my house. I could hear them yelling at me. Once I got on the porch, I turned and flicked them all off and screamed, "FUCK YOU!" it wasn't meant just for them; I was screaming at the entire world. That night, I closed and locked the front door for the first time.

Chapter 14

Randomly, Glenn would drop off a few groceries while we were asleep. Mainly a loaf of bread, ham, and tea. Afternoon showers were our savior from the heat. Practically every day, in the early afternoon, there would be a break from the exhausting heat. The sky would grow gray, and a slight breeze would kick up. I'd hurry around the house and put box fans in the windows. Alternating one facing in to pull air into the room and one facing out to suck air out. The air would start circulating within minutes, and the house would cool off.

This was the time of day when the kids and I would either nap or start cooking. We had no direction—not that we ever really did when my mother was home—but I felt lost. During that summer, I'd sometimes wake up before sunrise and sit on the front steps. I wondered how things could be this way. I was beyond lonely. I'd stare off into a daydream until the sun lit up the dewy grass, and the day would start all over again. I never remember my three younger siblings questioning what was going on. Somehow, they'd figured it out.

One night, I was sitting on the porch when the college guys who lived next door walked outside. "Hey, can you come and help us with the clutch?" The brown-haired guy with cargo shorts was harmless, and I knew it. The blond guy picked his head up from under the hood. He never seemed to pay me much attention. I flicked my cigarette from the front porch and walked over. My little brother stood on the porch in just a diaper with blond hair to his shoulders. The girls stood watching. Their haircuts were blunt and crooked because I'd also taken on the role of a barber.

"I don't know how to drive," I barked defensively.

"Just sit in the driver's seat and put it in gear," the brunette-haired guy said.

Embarrassed, I fumbled with the stick shift, pumping the pedals on the floorboard. Finally, the guy gestured to move over.

"How old are you?"

"Thirteen."

"Who lives with you in that house?"

"My mom and her husband."

"The guy who drives the truck, is that your boyfriend?"

"That's my stepdad." I laughed at him. I will never forget the look on his face that followed. Suddenly, he knew way more about me than I wanted him to.

"Then why does he stand and stare into your window at night." I stopped laughing. "Where's your mom? I haven't seen her in a few weeks."

My heart was pounding in my chest. A dark cloud covered my vision.

"She went on vacation, but she'll be back soon. What do you mean he looks in my window? He hasn't been here in days." I could feel my stomach turn inside out.

"He comes late after you're sleeping. Do you need anything?"

I walked away from him, humiliated and raging all at the same time. I needed to vomit, but the bile just lingered in my throat. The house was so hot I always slept without a shirt on; my mattress was under one of the windows in my room, which stayed open to let the air in. At that moment, everything crept up my spine and rested on my shoulders.

Chapter 15

Aunt Cara spent a few nights with me during my mom's jail time. One night, after I'd put the kids to bed, she was in my bathroom, showering. I was in the mirror in just my underwear. I was explaining I'd figured out how to use tampons. Mom handed me a box of tampons and told me to read the instructions, which I hadn't read. I inserted the entire pink plastic applicator and left it there. After a few days of dealing with the plastic rod poking me, I went to my mom. I explained I needed more pads because tampons hurt me.

"That's ridiculous. I put two in at once and didn't notice until I went to the doctor." Horrified that this could happen, I'd given up on tampons. Until the day I used my money to buy a box of OBs. I can't remember what made me do it besides the small box, so I assumed the tampons wouldn't hurt. When I took the first one out, I couldn't believe someone was smart enough to make such a thing. Sometime later, out of O.B. tampons, I reluctantly used my mom's tampons. Sitting on the toilet, anticipating the discomfort, I was about to insert the entire thing when I slipped and pushed the rod in too soon. And out popped an O.B. I was amazed; you weren't supposed to leave the pink plastic thing in, and that's why it hurt so badly. Cara laughed at me through the shower curtain. I thanked my mom aloud for giving me the pleasure of finding out how to use tampons the hard way.

In the corner of my eye, while looking in the mirror, I realized the door blocked from the kitchen and into my bathroom was cracked. My heart began pounding in my chest. My insides went into complete chaos. On the surface, I pretended not to notice. I quit talking and walked out like nothing was wrong. I continued out of my room into the kitchen. There he was. I hadn't seen him for days and had no idea how to contact him if there was an emergency. There he stood, wedged between the freezer and my bathroom door; his face was crammed so close to the crack the wood had to have been touching his face. He never realized I'd walked up to him; the view entranced him. At that moment, he was consumed by drugs. "Where the fuck have you been? What the fuck are you doing?" The rage escaped me, spilling out.

"I lost my keys, man. I thought they'd be behind here." He was sweaty and stumbled. Suddenly, I was embarrassed for him.

"Why are you looking in at me? They told me they saw you in my window." I was screaming and crying at the same time. I was humiliated. Mom was in jail, my dad wasn't around, and Glenn was so fucked up on drugs he was acting like a pervert. I became a thirteen-year-old mother to three kids. I wanted a parent. I needed a parent to take care of me. Instead, I was trying to survive in a world of mistakes made by adults who left me to navigate the consequences on my own.

He simply put his head down and stumbled out. I returned to my room and told Cara what happened. She left and didn't return. The next few days were a blur. When Glenn would come home, I'd ask if I could visit my mom. He always replied she didn't want visitors. I kept up with the kids and played house until she had served her time. Often, I'd wake before sunrise and sit on the front steps, admiring the cool morning air. I'd watch the dew on the grass, wondering why my life was so different.

Chapter 16

I had no idea when my mom was going to be released from the parish jail. We'd had no communication since the day she left. All that changed when I heard a knock at my bedroom door. I unlocked it, expecting to see my sisters or brother. By this time, I had cut my shoulder-length hair off into a chin-length bob and poured a bottle of Clorox on it, turning orange and brassy. I opened the door, and my mom was looking back at me. I was relieved to see her. I remember starting to lean forward, expecting to be embraced. Her hand slapped my face, leaving me stunned. I was completely caught off guard, still half asleep; the panic and rage sent me into a screaming match with her.

"You fucking slut!"

"What are you talking about?"

"Oh, he fucking told me how you took off the minute I went in. He had to take care of the kids and had no idea where you were. You kept him from going to school. You fucking little bitch."

"What? He didn't know where I was?" At this point, I was screaming at the top of my lungs, gasping for air. "Why don't you ask him what the fuck he was doing peeking into my bathroom?" I was frantic. "Ask the neighbor who he sees looking in my fucking window at night. Ask your husband what happened to his keys to the house."

I sobbed. What else was there to do? I longed for her

to console me. She turned and screamed into her room, where he lay on the bed. He never admitted or denied any of it. He lay there silently, and she never mentioned it again, nor was there any apology.

After she got out of jail, my mom's habits changed. It was the summer before I was to start high school; she began dumpster diving. I think it was partly to have some independence, something to do. Unable to drive, she was at the mercy of someone so messed up half of the time he couldn't function. If Glenn wouldn't oblige her with a ride, she'd jump on her bicycle and head out to sift through garbage in dumpsters. She started bringing home everything from shoes to lipstick for me. Eventually, she befriended the neighborhood veteran dumpster diver, an older man who had a hard time keeping his dirty hands to himself around little girls. He'd come over to bring designer treasures he found during his daily rounds. He'd park his cruiser bike in our front yard with black trash bags tied to it and bring random items to our mom. I wanted to vanish into thin air when I walked down the street and saw my mom climbing in and out of a dumpster. The embarrassment did not keep me from accepting the partially used treasures. My room soon became filled with partially used makeup pallets, clothes that didn't quite fit, and other random items pulled from dumpsters—some engraved with names like Sara or Stacy. I simply turned the things around so the name would not be visible and then claimed them as my own. She rode her bike religiously from dumpster to dumpster. If she wasn't picking through dumpsters, she was collecting aluminum cans. We lived near the university; the strip of bars the college kids flocked to was not far from our house. Bags of aluminum cans lined the side of our house. When she returned home from collecting cans, my little sisters were tasked with smashing them. They would jump and stomp on the cans to flatten them. Eventually, she would load up the black trash bags in the bed of Glenn's two-seater Toyota, and they'd sell them for cash.

My mother stayed in her room more than before. Glenn slept most of the day and disappeared at night. When he woke, he poured himself a tall glass of Coke and Jim Beam. At night, Mom started taking tranquilizers to sleep. Visitors stopped in to make a purchase. Since her time in jail, she had become even more selective about whom she dealt with, and only a few were allowed to purchase from her.

One night, while lip-synching to the radio, I was washing dishes when I turned around and saw a man watching me. "You the dryer man?" I asked.

"No." He was skinny, with thin blond hair. "You were waiting on the dryer, man?"

"Yeah, it's broken."

"No, I'm Glenn's study buddy."

I laughed at him. He looked at me like he was studying me. I felt awkward and exposed. Eddie began asking me questions about where I went to school and what I did for fun. Not knowing how to answer questions about myself, I felt stupid. I wanted to get away from him. There was something about him that made me feel vulnerable. Eddie came over more and more frequently. He and Glenn began renting out small refrigerators to the dorms on the campus. Something Eddie had done for some time, and he needed help to haul them. Glenn started to assist Eddie with his side hustle. They met in a nursing class at the university. This meant Eddie was over often. He'd come into my room and ask me about my school grades.

"What did you make on your report card?"

I thought he was so weird. No one asked me about school. I forged my mom's signature on most things, good or bad, to avoid hearing her scream.

"I don't know, a C in English, an F in Math, and an A- in Home Ec." He reached into his wallet and tossed cash onto my bed. I was confused.

"Let me know what your next report card says. I always pay my kids for their grades. Make A's, and I will pay you. I don't care what subject it is. You want to go swimming tomorrow?"

Eddie showed up on his motorcycle the next day and took me to a health club. I had never been in a place like that before. I was speechless. People were walking around, smiling and talking. No one was smoking or angry. More than anything, I felt relaxed as I lay in the sunlight with sweat dripping down my skin. The smell of chlorine was intoxicating. Eddie mentioned he had two younger kids, a boy, and a girl. He asked if I'd babysit while he and his wife went out.

At their house, everything was calm. Eddie and his wife would go out, and I spent the night babysitting. Eddie paid me generously, and I could get out of my house for a few hours. I needed this reprieve to cope with the things at home. Eddie wanted to know my plans after high school. I just wanted to make money. He planted the notion in my head that education equates to money. Eddie also started chanting something to me about breaking the cycle.

"You don't want to be like them."

"No."

"Then stay in school and make good grades."

Eddie showed up one afternoon as I was sitting in my room with the box fans vibrating in my window. I didn't know how he figured out when I needed things, but I'd been asked to homecoming.

"Isn't homecoming in a few weeks?"

"Yes. This guy asked me to go, but I don't have a dress, and she won't give me any money for one." I nodded towards my mom's room.

He tossed a wad of cash on my bed. I didn't expect him to give me money; no one had ever done something like that for me. Eddie tried to give me a glimpse of normalcy, a tiny rope to hang onto. He picked me up and took me places I'd never been. He exposed me to a lifestyle other than what I knew, and because of him, I knew life could be very different. Eddie gave me a sense of self-worth, for which I am forever grateful.

Chapter 17

One of Glenn's favorite escapes was the swampy basin. He'd spend most nights in the basin. Once, he came home with a beige-colored sack full of snakes. Walking into the bathroom, with the single light bulb hanging above my head and a pull string dangling in front of my face, I saw the bathtub filled with a couple of inches of water. Inside were more snakes than I cared to count, swimming around. He stood watching them. Sometimes, my heart beats so fast, pumping all of my blood so quickly, that I become extremely hot and cold at the same time. After walking out, it didn't take long to hear Mom screaming to get them out of the house.

Despite Mom not working, I was responsible for most of the housework—dishes, laundry, sometimes cooking, and looking after the kids. I hated going outside to our small shed, where the washer and dryer were. The shed had a screen door and an extremely narrow walkway. It was hot, dirty, and too small. I always picked up my pace to get in and out as fast as possible.

One afternoon, I walked outside to transfer the wet laundry into the dryer. I remember the intense heat; it followed me wherever I went. The shed's heat and mustiness made breathing hard with the added hot air from the dryer. I walked up to the screen door, pulling it open. As I stepped in, an aquarium caught my eye to my immediate right. The walkway was so narrow that the aquarium was inches from my arm. I stood, curious, trying to figure out what was in it. It seemed like one of those optical illusions where I'd have to let my eyes go unfocused to see the hidden picture in the dots. Finally, I saw the image; it was a copperhead snake looking right back at me. On top of the aquarium was a screen held down by a brick.

Fear pricked my flesh, horror at the thought of facing this thing each time I came to the laundry room. My blood raced, and I started to sweat. I finally got to the washer. The heat was causing the chemical smell of paint thinner to fill the shed. Something inside of me wanted to smell it more. I grabbed the can of thinner off the shelf and inhaled the fumes. Within seconds, I was light-headed I felt like I was floating. What was most appealing was how extremely calm I became. Each day, I summoned enough courage to get past that snake. I rewarded myself by sitting on the washing machine, shoving my nose into the rectangle can of toxic chemicals, and inhaling as deeply as possible. I huffed for so long that black clouds would roll over my eyesight. With my eyes wide open, I'd only see blackness. I started seeing commercials with public service announcements that huffing was a lack of oxygen to my brain. Not wanting to die, I stopped.

Chapter 18

Summer began to wind down, and the anxiety of starting high school set in. I felt like an outcast around kids my age. Over the summer, while Mom was in jail, I'd hung around older people no longer in school. I felt out of place and looked even more out of place. I didn't have the clothes teenagers wore. My clothes didn't fit and were pulled from a dumpster. Hoping an invisible switch would flip. I fantasized about Mom reassuring me everything would be ok and sending me off with positive words of encouragement. But that didn't happen. She was too consumed with her husband, who now slept all day and began blacking out from his intravenous drug habit. She'd scream at him, and he still wouldn't budge. I realized he was spending lots of time in the bathroom.

He became increasingly cruel towards Crystal. It was nothing for her to have to stay in the hallway for hours with no air conditioner or fan. Eventually, I started to show my anger towards how she was treated. The other two kids just stayed out of the house, out of the way. If I saw Crystal sitting for too long, I'd tell her to get up or put a fan in front of her. Eventually, her smile faded, and she seemed to go somewhere else in her mind.

"Where is it?" It was not unusual for Mom to rant and rave, screaming and hollering about something being stolen. She was screaming at Glenn. As he lay there on his back, he didn't budge. "I know you have something. Where is it?" The old wooden radio blared from another room, and a soft rock station of the 70s and 80s music played in the background.

I developed a survival instinct. I could observe my surroundings, which allowed me to piece together clues through some sixth sense. I got up off my bed that day and walked to the bathroom. I climbed on the bathtub's edge and stood on my tippy toes, stretching up so high to reach the top of the cabinet. I had no idea how I knew it was there. I certainly never saw what he did in the bathroom. I have no way to explain it other than I just knew. I felt around until I knew I'd found it. His stash of needles and whatever it was he was shooting up. I took it down and brought it to my mom. I don't remember if she did it or if I did, but one of us threw the pouch, needles, and all in the storm drain across the street. Pretending that would keep him off the stuff. That's when I knew things were only going to get worse.

The reality that Glenn was shooting up brought out a different level of rage in my mother, which never went back to wherever it came from. Her anger permeated through the walls of our house. I only remember her being happy when an occasional girlfriend stopped by to buy a bag. On a good day, her ceiling fan would be on full blast. I remember a mustard-yellow sheet on top of her waterbed, and she'd sit Indian-style, with one leg bent so her heel faced her back. She and her girlfriend would talk about men and have other chitchat conversations. Still slender and tan at that time, she'd push her hair behind her ears. She had a loud belly laugh that only made its way out of her on rare occasions during this time in our lives.

Moments like this, I knew I could creep in and sit quietly in the wicker rocking chair at the foot of her bed without her yelling at me about some random chore I didn't complete. Her girlfriends always treated me as if I were an adult. I can still hear the faint tapping of the beaded ceiling fan chain gently touching the side of the frosted globe covering the light bulb. They'd pass a joint back and forth, snorting while choking between giggles. I felt calm in those moments. I still hated that I couldn't have friends over, but at least she was happy in those short moments. I would sacrifice having my own company any day as long as my mom was content.

After much persuasion, she'd give in to her friend's request for her to read their tarot cards. She acted like she didn't want to, always claiming she didn't want to see any bad stuff ahead of them. Once everyone was good and high, she'd reach back and grab the green tin can at the head of her bed. The green tin can all of us kids knew better than to mess with. The lack of circulation from her closed windows, on top of the absence of an air conditioner, made it one stagnant, stuffy, thick fog of smoke.

Once she opened the tin, she carefully unwrapped the deck of tarot cards from the handkerchief that kept the cards quietly and safely protected from the world. The process began with the ritual of halving the deck, allowing the person to handle the cards, and finally, after a long time, the process concluded with her grabbing the book and deciphering the meaning of life. In those moments, she was mystical and well. Looking back, maybe it was because she felt a sense of purpose. Now that I think about it, had I been brave enough to ball up next to her and put my head on her knee, she may have even caressed me. Funny how I never did, and she never reached out to pull me close.

One night, while lying in my bed with the box fans on full blast, I was just starting to cool down with the summer evening. I lay with my radio and fans on, drifting off to sleep, when I heard a commotion outside my room. Followed by shrill screams of her calling Glenn a motherfucker and more screaming. My heart began to wear itself out. Moments later, as I was expecting the meltdown to pass, she started wailing for me over and over, "V, V, come quick."

I pulled a shirt over my head and turned the deadbolt on my bedroom door. He was lying flat on his back, pale and looking close to dead. She was kneeling over him in a sheer white cotton gown. She gathered it up in one hand while looking up at me, her hair a tangled mess.

"Help him. I think he shot up too much of that shit. Help him, I think he's gonna die."

I stood looking down at him. I didn't know what else to say

but "Let him die."

In my teenage mind, the life he was living was like being dead already. I turned and bolted my door shut as she began screaming, for not only the neighbors but the gods themselves to hear I was a fucking slut, over and over again. I don't remember how he survived that night. I only knew that I had to get out of the house.

Chapter 19

I dreaded the start of school. Besides having no proper clothes, I knew Mom would flip out when I brought home a list of school fees and supplies I needed. Mom had a locked cedar armoire; only her skeleton key opened it. Inside, she kept everything from weed to money and snacks. She hid her key from Glenn to keep him from using her money for drugs. Instinctively, I knew where she hid it, in her old Army jacket pocket. I began helping myself to cash here and there, including much of my school fee money. Teachers didn't take pity on kids who didn't have the money. Instead, I picked up on the condescending comments they murmured under their breath or the sideways glances they passed our way when they went down the list of students who still hadn't paid. In addition, I mastered forging my mom's signature, but not because I was afraid to show her my grades. Instead, she would get pissed off that she had to stop watching her soap operas to sign the papers or read the forms the school sent home. Rather than deal with that, I signed my own papers and report cards not to bother her when I knew she was not in the mood to deal with me.

The first day of high school was terrifying, and I've had some pretty scary times. I stood outside and didn't recognize a soul. I didn't have a mom or dad wrapping me in self-confidence when I stepped out for my first day of high school. I stood in the commons area, watching the groups of kids as my heart thumped so loud the vibrations made me light-headed. I was wearing floral-print jeans, which were not trendy at all. They were hand-me-downs from a forty-year-old woman.

On that first day, I attracted a couple of seniors. Craving attention, I was giddy when my phone started ringing. Little did I know then I was simply an easy target for older guys who were raging with hormones. A few days later, I eagerly accepted the idea to "go out" with my first boyfriend, Chad. It didn't take long to end up at his house. He had his own car; I instantly loved leaving the house. I had a getaway. He could have been anyone, and I would still have been in love. I was free, which was the best feeling in the world. I had to be careful. If I let him into my house for too long, he would surely see the dysfunction and hear Mom screaming and hollering. He would smell the constant aroma of weed. He'd see the people coming into her room to buy it.

Chad was expected to graduate and head out to college. The *real me* was not something he would want, much less be allowed to date. I was only fourteen. Walking into his house for the first time was mesmerizing. It was immaculate—the air fresh, crisp. I stepped into the largest kitchen I'd ever seen. The living room was to the left and had a television. I marveled. Not only that but the entire family was seated on the couch and loveseat, watching TV and hanging out.

I grew uncomfortable as I stood there with all eyes on me. Chad's parents sat inspecting the prize. He nudged me to have a seat. I didn't belong there. My face grew hot and red. I fidgeted, wanting to return to the insanity I understood and was comfortable with. What would I say when his mom or dad asked how my family made a living?

Luckily, I don't remember the conversation. I learned that my new boyfriend was very possessive, which was completely fine with me. For once, someone was taking care of me. I loathed when he dropped me off at home on Sunday evenings. As I walked up the steps, my veins seemed to fill with lead, pulling me down. My chest tightened as I opened the screen door; the intense heat blanketed my body, making breathing hard.

On several occasions, when I walked into the house, Crystal was in some type of punishment. On this day, she was sitting at the table, her blonde hair brown tight around her face from sweat, ringlets clinging to her wet skin, her head bobbing up and down, left and right. Her little brown eyes closed as her muscles tried to sleep in peace. Sitting in front of her was broiled meat and lumpy mashed potatoes. For such a little thing, she was stubborn. Looking above her head, I glanced out the blinds to see Rose and David playing in the yard. David was only wearing a diaper as usual—his hair now past his shoulders. I marched into Mom's room.

"How long has she been sitting there?" My heart raced. Fed up with her getting the brunt of Glenn's punishments, I was confrontational and demanding an explanation. I glared at my mother while she lay on the mustard-yellow sheet that covered her waterbed, watching her soap operas while Glenn was passed out. The ceiling fan made a faint knocking noise, swirling the hot air into a humid breeze.

"Where have you been?" she said, taking a hit off her roach clip.

"You can't allow him to keep hurting her like this." I was screaming. My insides were cracking and coming apart. Panic filled my nerves, and again, I trembled. I stomped back to Crystal and picked up her plate. She was ordered to sit there until she ate the food but she refused. The food was dried out and cold.

"Get up!" I barked. She was startled awake and scurried off outside. I walked into the kitchen and hurled the plate into the sink. Dishes were piled up. Despite-always being gone, I was still responsible for cleaning up. I cranked the radio loudly and started washing, scrubbing, and tossing dishes into the drainboard.

The following day, I woke up and knew something wasn't right. Before I moved, I could feel a knot in my stomach. Dread flooded my body. Something was wrong. I heard someone awake in the kitchen, which never happened. Usually, the girls and I got up alone and got ready for school. No one saw us off in the morning.

Walking into the kitchen, I saw Glenn bent over and stirring constantly at the stove. At first, I was confused and tinged with satisfaction that he got up to cook us breakfast. Finally, someone was ready to help me and see us off before school. I walked closer and realized he didn't see me, even though he should have. It was our smallest pan, the one I used to melt butter. I stood next to him, and he never looked up or at me. I don't think he could see anything. He was entirely out of it.

He stared down and stirred, sweat dripping down his nose. Acid rose in my throat as the walls of my neck constricted. Shear panic ran through my blood; my heart pumped rapidly, and I began to get tunnel vision. Chad would be pulling up any minute; if he came in and saw this, he'd never speak to me again. He knew things weren't right, but he had no idea how wrong they were. The girls would be waking soon, and they'd see this. I didn't want to deal with this shit. Rose walked up to her dad, but he didn't see her. Crystal stood next to the stove and stared into the pan at the mixture he was carefully tending. I watched her; she was blank. Whatever was being cooked in that little was going to end up in a syringe, and I wanted all of us out of the house before that happened.

"Get dressed," I barked. I was overburdened with caring for them and often vented my frustrations. Together, they did as they were told.

My next memory flashes to getting inside Chad's car. He had a breakfast burrito for me. My stomach was still flipping, and food was the last thing on my mind. Things were going too far, and Glenn's drug use was intense. I knew that made things dangerous. Pulling up at school was dreadful. Chad loved school and made straight A's in all his advanced classes. I was failing. In class, I felt inadequate, as if everyone knew how messed up my life was. I had missed so much school that I was always behind from being truant.

I sat in the back of the classroom and tried to look busy in my notebook, which usually consisted of me writing free-verse poetry. My heart raced when the teacher asked students to read or answer questions. Sitting through a lesson was like everyone spoke a foreign language. Sitting through a math class was torture —looking at the equations was like an abstract picture—I couldn't find a solution. After a while, I grew too embarrassed to ask for help.

Day after day, the teacher stood at her projector and worked problem after problem. I couldn't do the work. I'd fallen too far behind. I remember teachers looking disgusted when I didn't complete a homework assignment. I wanted to. More than anything, I fantasized about turning in assignments. When I left school and got home, I was too tired, hot, busy, or in the middle of a nervous breakdown from screaming matches with Mom. Completing an assignment was not on my priority list. I made answers up for a while, thinking I had a chance of getting them right. Eventually, I quit doing that, too.

That afternoon, when Chad dropped me off after school, I pulled the door open to the house and knew something was wrong. I could smell the thick and intoxicating aroma of Mr. Clean. The entire house was spotless, clean, and dusted; this made no sense. I walked to the kitchen and saw a large box of Popeye's fried chicken on the stove. We never had take-out, not the kids. Mom stood in the kitchen. She tried to smile, but she was still shaken. I wanted to hug her for the first time in a long time, but I didn't know how. I stood looking at her I was confused.

Eventually, she told me after we left that morning, Glenn went "crazy" and started tearing the house apart, smashing things, emptying all-the food onto the floor, completely out of his mind. Whatever he had cooked up messed him up badly. I had told her what he was doing that morning before we left for school. I was OK up until that point. I was trying to process and decide how to fix it. Then she lifted her shirt and showed me how he'd gotten after her with the broom handle. This made no sense to me as if I were watching a movie. As strange as their relationship was, they had never gotten physically violent with each other. Rage filled my soul. I ran and charged into their bedroom. I didn't realize Chad had returned and was standing in the living room the entire time.

He witnessed the part of my life I tried to hide from the world.

I slammed on the light, yanking the beaded cord so hard I anticipated the glass globe to shatter. Glenn was on their waterbed, sweating in a cold sleep. I startled him awake, but he lay there pretending not to be.

"You fucking piece of shit. Do you want to fucking hit somebody? Huh?" At this point, I think I started hitting him, but, to be completely honest, I blacked out. "I fucking hate you. I wish you would die. Don't touch her again! Any of them!! You fucking hear me!"

I wish we could have punched the sickness out of each other. I just wanted us to feel love. I wanted the screaming and verbal abuse to stop. More than anything, I wanted a mom I could hang out with, like most girls my age, and a stepdad who didn't shoot up. He didn't give me the satisfaction of even moving that day. He just lay there sweating while I came undone.

Then I heard Chad's voice. I wanted to disappear. He'd know everything now. I'd be stuck with no out. I told him everything. Well, not about the needles and cooking drugs, almost everything. Within a few months, Chad graduated and joined a fraternity. He moved on to sorority girls. I was stuck—no more weekend getaways, sitting in his living room eating pizza with his family—no more. I was going to be home every day.

Chapter 20

Depression was a black blanket thrown over me, and I had to figure out how to get from under it. Every ounce of energy pulled away from me. Something went off inside of me. I pulled my hand-me-down queen-sized bed apart and dragged it to the road. I rearranged things in my room. I slept on the hardwood floor. I cried for days, not able to get out of bed except to use the bathroom. I suppose I ate at some point. I didn't talk on the phone or care about anything. Not one time did any adult open my door to see about me. Never did Mom show any concern. I slipped into a debilitating darkness. There was no trip to the doctor for medication or a storybook breakthrough with help. None of those things happened. The darkness was kind enough to lift itself, and I crawled out of bed one day.

As a sophomore, I had a friend who drove. Entertainment for me on the weekends consisted of going to keg parties and drinking in open sugar cane fields. In my steamy room, I'd stand before the full-length mirror on my wall and apply too much makeup. An old jam box sat on my dresser, salvaged from the trash. A can of yams balanced on the power button to keep it on, and a wire coat hanger served as the antenna. I'd crank the radio until the speakers rattled. I was never asked to turn my music down; we all had a love for music.

Lining my eyes with charcoal liner, I darted back and forth from the freezer to my room. Standing with my head in the freezer to keep my makeup from melting in the heat, I'd glance up and see my two sisters sitting on their bottom bunk bed, looking at me with blank expressions. I knew they were bored; they needed attention. The door to Mom and Glenn's room was already closed and locked for the night, with the light from the television peeking under the door. I'd hear the roach clip tinging on the glass ashtray's edge. My heart swelled, looking at the girls—their hair damp from sweat and the open windows only letting in the sound of the cicadas and the traffic flowing by.

"Go in my room and watch TV while I'm gone." I didn't say it warmly, but they were pleased, and their feet patted quickly across the wooden floor. Soon, the horn was honking through the house. The screen door slammed behind me. In the hatchback, we'd head out for the night. I felt free as my arm dangled out the open window with a lit Marlboro.

The night progressed as it usually did, with a trail of cars full of teenagers ready for a night of drinking and fun. We ended up at a house in a rich neighborhood, and another set of parents gone for the weekend. A person sat at the front door, collecting the $5 entry fee. My Solo cup was filled with cheap keg beer. I aimlessly wandered from group to group.

At a party like this, I met the next guy I dated briefly. He had already graduated from high school. I don't recall how I introduced him to my mom. He eventually began taking my mom's cash to purchase weed for her in large quantities. I'd ride with him to the house where he'd buy Mom's supply. The man and his wife were old enough to be my parents. The woman sat on her throne of a bed, just like my mom. She took out the scales and weighed Mom's portion. We smoked too many joints for me to keep track of, and he rolled up Mom's portion and shoved it in the waistband of his shorts.

Night after night, we'd party. We loaded up in a friend's car one night and went to a new apartment. I remember feeling high and was not interested in getting any more messed up. I was the only girl with about five or six college guys. Sitting around on the couch, the guy who lived in the apartment rolled a joint and bragged about its potency. I sat with men's tube socks up to my knees, bright red stripes on each knee, cutoff shorts, and a Sunday school T-shirt.

The guy passed the joint my way, and I shook my head no. Even that young, I was cautious not to mess with hard stuff. I knew what addiction did, and I wanted no part of that. The joint stayed in front of me—I had to take a pull—this guy wouldn't take no for an answer. I knew there was something in it, but I smoked it anyway, wanting to get it over with.

Moments later, my heart began racing. I was skittish and hyper. The guys went back to the kitchen to play Spades. I couldn't sit still. I asked if we could go for a ride to get me out of the apartment. He slid his keys to the car over to me. Nervous, not knowing what to do with myself, I grabbed them and walked to the parking lot. It was drizzling, and I had only driven a couple of times but never on my own, not to mention I was too high.

Still determined that driving a stick shift couldn't be all that hard, I jumped in. I only remember parts of what happened next. Driving through a neighborhood, I got confused with the clutch and ended up in a ditch—not completely—but enough to feel like the vehicle was stuck. I began trying to reverse out repeatedly, but I had no idea what I was doing. My heart thumped over and over. I ran to the house across the street and banged on the door. I can only imagine what I looked like to the woman who answered: high, soaking wet from the rain, and rambling nonstop. The woman told me she couldn't drive a standard. I don't know how I did it, but somehow, I got that car out of the ditch and made it back to the apartment alive and without being arrested. Eventually, I stopped seeing him.

Chapter 21

I was in my mother's bathroom one day. She began banging on the door, telling me to hurry up. I finished using the restroom and walked out. Screaming at me, "You have your own fucking bathroom."

I was confused about what the big deal was. Trying not to escalate the situation, I walked past Mom into my bedroom. Her insults still reverberated. "I don't want you using my toilet. You will give me AIDS, you nasty little bitch."

Speechless, I didn't scream back. I just fell onto the edge of my bed and bargained with God to help me find a way out. We screamed back and forth. I felt depleted, a complete void of anything good. Something as simple as using the bathroom sent her into a rage, using words that lashed into my being. I silently wondered if I had AIDS. Maybe she knew something I didn't. Her irrational accusations made me obsess about the thought I could have AIDS.

"I want you out of my fucking house, you whore," she screamed in my face—spit flying out of her mouth.

"Fuck you!" was all I could reply, shaking and breaking apart. I could hear Glenn whispering to her in their room. She screamed for me to get out over and over. Not knowing what else to do, I grabbed a garbage bag and filled it with clothes. I was nauseous, wanting to vomit.

"Shut up!!" I screamed over and over. I wanted to cover

my ears. I didn't want to hear her scream anymore. I just wanted her screaming to stop. I desperately wanted silence. I ran out barefoot. A few houses down, I knocked on the door of a girl I knew. She lived alone with her mom and older sister. I went into her room and cried out my story. Staying there was not option; I didn't even bother asking. I just needed a place to calm down and think. Eventually, I called Aunt Cara. She was now in her twenties and lived with her boyfriend. She picked me up.

Arriving at her one-bedroom apartment, I knew deep in my belly it wouldn't work. She and her soon-to-be husband didn't exactly welcome me with open arms. I felt like a burden, placing my garbage bag of clothes in the corner behind the coffee table. I hoped it would be out of sight, out of mind—to extend my stay. I slept on the living room floor and tried to be invisible. I went to school during the day and worked most nights. Getting to and from school was as stressful as crashing on the floor. I constantly needed a ride but somehow managed.

While in class one day, I was called to the front office. My chest began pounding as my sneakers squeaked on the waxed floor with every step. A few weeks earlier, the principal had suspended me for hanging birthday flyers around campus for a friend. At the time, it wasn't a big deal. It was just a prank to embarrass my friend. According to the principal, the problem was that I taped them on the green-painted poles around campus. He claimed I damaged school property because the tape pulled off the paint when the signs were removed. Things got out of hand when he said he would call my mom. I knew she'd scream at him on the phone, which was more embarrassing than I could handle. I tried to bargain and offered to repaint the poles, but he refused. At some point, I lost it. I started screaming and crying in his office, completely irrational. He sat across from me dumbfounded, like I was a foreign object he'd never seen before. I cursed and screamed out of panic. I just didn't want anyone else to hear my mother scream about me being a whore or slut. When he called, I got quiet and could hear my mother from across his desk. Quietly, he set the receiver down and excused me from his office.

As I rounded the corner to the attendance office in the front of the school, I saw Aunt Cara standing there with her car keys in her hand; she wasn't smiling.

"What's up?" I asked

"V, you can't stay with us anymore." She had no expression on her face.

"Why?"

"You just can't. He doesn't think it's a good idea." She turned and walked towards the front door, leaving me standing there. I had nowhere else to go. I rode the bus home that afternoon. When I walked in, it was like I had never left. This happened many times over the years. I'd get thrown out and leave for as long as I could, but I would always have to go back.

My mom screamed not only at us kids but at Glenn as well. She accused him of having affairs regularly. He would disappear for days. He tried to do anything he could to stay out of the house. If Mom needed something from the store, she ensured he took her instead of sending him alone, not knowing if he'd ever return. Occasionally, he took me with him to get out without her. Most of the time, we rode through a nearby neighborhood, where Glenn would crank up Alice In Chains and let me drive aimlessly through the neighborhoods. Essentially, he could just relax. We'd ride around for hours, silent while the music blared. He had a few friends who lived on the college campus, and sometimes we'd stop by. We'd go into an apartment where the guys were young, high, and intelligent. I was never uncomfortable there; I knew they wouldn't do anything in front of me. I'd be offered a beer and sit on the couch while Glenn followed them into a back bedroom. I never went back there and never asked what was going on. I watched MTV music videos while waiting for him to walk back out slowly.

Most of the time, I could hear my mom stomping on the hardwood floors as I climbed out of the car when we got home from those late-night drives. If she was pissed, she started screaming before we walked up the steps to the porch. If she weren't pissed, I'd only hear her roach clip chiming against her glass ashtray.

Chapter 22

A t school, I continued to struggle just to show up. I desperately wanted to be there, like the other kids. I remember how the others seemed to have extended family at school. The cheerleaders and athletes worked in the office and often felt comfortable hanging out in their teachers' classes. This was sometime in my sophomore year. The more school I missed, the farther behind I got. Leaving me disconnected from the routines and my ability to keep up with academics. Not wanting to stand out, I'd make myself look busy by journaling or writing poetry during lessons.

While sitting in class one day, I was paged to go to the front office. Confused, I got up, wondering what I had done. The office clerk nodded toward the phone receiver. I reached for it. Why would I have a phone call?

"Hello?" I could hear her breathing before she even spoke. I knew Mom was on the other line.

"Venus, did you leave the shed open last night?" I remember standing there, frozen. Her breathing was heavy. My mind was trying to process the question.

"What? What are you talking about?" I tried desperately to cup my hand around the bottom of the receiver to muffle her voice, knowing that everyone in the office could hear her. Then she started screaming. My chest immediately started pounding. My skin was hot and cold at the same time. A blur of Kelly green letterman jackets filled the office.

"You fucking little bitch! You left the shed unlocked, and they stole my fucking bike . . . "

I couldn't let her finish. I slammed the receiver down as my chest heaved. Everyone in the office stopped, just like in a movie, and it felt like time froze. The entire office was speechless, staring at me. I turned and walked out as they whispered. If the ground beneath me had cracked open and allowed me to fall in, I would have been relieved.

Chapter 23

The last summer, I visited my dad before he was sent to prison. I had a new stepmom, and things changed. There was a sternness in him that was foreign to me. When he got off work, he barely acknowledged me. The new stepmom was nothing like Dana, my first stepmom. Dana treated me like she looked forward to having me around. This new wife, Tina, made me feel uncomfortable. I was unsure what had happened between him and Dana that led them to divorce. I only picked up bits and pieces while listening to my aunt talk. All I could piece together at that point was there were issues with drugs and money.

In the meantime, Tina assured me she would rescue Dad from his legal problems. She explained she worked for his lawyer. Tina had a teenage son with whom my father constantly had it out. The summer was long, and his distance from me made me uneasy. He was living in a trailer in the middle of nowhere in North Texas. There was nothing around but dirt roads and gravel. During the day, I watched television and rode aimlessly around with my new stepbrother. We sat in his room for hours together, smoking Marlboro Reds while playing video games. He kept my mind off the changes.

While playing video games one evening, I heard my dad's tires grinding into the gravel driveway. When he entered the trailer, the usual sound of his car keys falling onto the counter followed. I could hear his deep exhale of cigarette smoke as he walked through the living room. Suddenly, the door to the bedroom opened; we sat on the floor with remote controls to the Nintendo in our hands, Mario & Luigi bouncing in the air. Before I could ask how his day was, the two of them were outside—Dad shouting at him to keep his fucking hands off me. My chest grew tight. I wanted to run out and help the boy, but I didn't want to challenge Dad. Maybe it was because I'd seen him react to other men while he was drunk or high at biker parties, or it could be the stories my mom had told me. As listened through the walls that afternoon, for the first time, I wanted to go home. I didn't understand what he was going through. I thought everything was about me. As an adult, I realized Dad's anger wasn't about my stepbrother. It wasn't me. My dad was facing prison time and didn't know how to cope with his emotions. Instead, we all began to build unnecessary walls not understanding how to talk about what was happening.

Days later, Tina told me he would be going to prison for a crime he'd committed while still married to Dana. He bought me a plane ticket to fly home. My dad was gone, and I had no idea how long he would be incarcerated or why this was happening. Sure, he'd get rowdy at parties with the rest of his friends, but prison? He wasn't capable of doing anything to deserve that.

Devastated, I returned home to my mom. Usually, I was refreshed when I returned and ready to mother my siblings; this time, I returned in pieces. When I walked through the rusted screen door and was greeted with a wave of incense smoke mixed in with the heavy stench of weed and cigarette smoke, I wondered what I had ever done for God to give me the family he did. Why do some kids get a family that will nurture and love them and others don't? I cried, not knowing when I'd see Dad again.

With her hair pinned up and wearing a white flannel nightgown, Mom greeted me as she asked for the latest update on Dad. In a dreamy voice, she'd say, "I'll always love that man."

I grew to loathe this statement because the inquisition wasn't to comfort me or probe me for my feelings; it was to gather information on my dad, whom she never got over. Delusional is an accurate way to describe my mother and her memories of time with my dad.

I remember a screaming match between the two of us; I couldn't stand to hear her proclaim her love for him and, in the following sentence, describe how he beat her regularly those many years ago when they were still married. Over and over, my mother explained how he would punch her and kick her around when I was an infant. It seemed almost as if I bore the burden of his abuse. I didn't want to hear her stories. I just wanted to have a dad without anyone telling me the horrible things he might have done when he was younger. She almost seemed invigorated when recalling her past with him.

Soon after that last visit with Dad, Michelle, a girl I met at school, picked me up and said she was going to look for a job in the mall. A job—that's a way to make money and get on my own. Something started pumping inside me. Together we walked the mall.

"I don't even know why I'm doing this. I won't have a ride to work."

"Won't your stepdad bring you?" she asked.

"Probably not."

"My parents said I have to get a job."

We walked up to a store; the windows were covered with brown paper. There were boxes everywhere filled with clothes.

"What kind of store is this going to be?" Michelle asked.

"A clothing store for young adults. How old are you?" a woman with a sharp nose asked.

"Sixteen," I snapped, defensive and insecure.

"You'll need a worker's permit."

I looked at Michelle, doubtful. On the way home, Michelle explained how to get the permit and even offered to give me a ride if we worked the same shift. I was hopeful this would work out. Making money—maybe I could finally save enough to get my own place.

Like most times when I came close to seeing the light, black clouds quickly rolled. That night, when I got home, I opened my mother's door to her bedroom to tell her my good news. This was it: I would make money, save, buy a car, and do something. Something different. My mother didn't drive and seemed so helpless—always in the house, waiting for a ride or having to ride her bicycle. I could buy school clothes and things I needed as a teenager. I thought she'd be proud. I stood in her doorway and rambled about needing a worker's permit. Could Glenn help me out with a very now and then? I'd even help out with gas.

She became outraged; she was like an animal frothing at the mouth. She screamed at me. How could I do this to her? Once again, I was a stupid fucking bitch; she'd lose her medical card for me. If I worked, she'd have to report my income and lose whatever food stamps or welfare she was collecting. I was a whore and a slut. Eventually, I became just as vicious and screamed back, hating every breath I took. Deflated and empty, I retreated to my room, boxed in and panicking. I started throwing my belongings in a black bag, and shallow breaths intensified my panic.

"Just get the fuck out," she spewed at me. Her long hair tangled. She'd stomp out and slam her door.

"Fuck this!" I shoved things into a trash bag. My sisters huddled together on the bottom bunk of their beds, keeping quiet and waiting to see what would happen next.

I lost count of how often I took off or got kicked out of the house once I started high school. I'd crash on the couch of friends until I'd get the hint from their parents that it was time to go. Usually, the first place I went was downtown, but I grew tired and begged a neighbor to go inside her house. Usually, someone's parents would call the cops, and they'd pick me up and bring me back home. Each time, I could read the cop's expression like he knew something wasn't right. He just didn't know what to do about it. The truth is, I honestly wanted to lie down and die during this point in my life. Being only a sophomore in high school, I was too young to support myself and live independently. I was exhausted, continuously hearing my mom scream at me. I started to feel transparent and just wanted to vanish. I would have willingly laid flat on the ground and become part of the earth. Still and calm, at peace. No more panic, no more disappointment.

Thanks to Michelle, I got the job in the mall. I knew making money would be the only way to support myself. That first day of work gave me a sense of purpose and drive. The store was being put together. We unpacked box after box of clothes, shoes, hats, jewelry, you name it. I was overwhelmed by so much stuff I couldn't afford. Working made me feel important. I had a focus. It consumed my thoughts and was an escape. I fell in love with working; my mind was free. The older woman in charge excitedly said we would open that night. I remember how unexpected that was. We weren't supposed to open for at least another day, but we set the store up in less time than expected. I thought I'd get to hide in the back and continue with the manual labor of unpacking and organizing. She asked me if I had any other clothes. I shook my head no. I was thin, in old jeans and a worn-out flannel shirt. I wasn't wearing any makeup. She said stand here, pointing to the front doors from which we had just pulled the brown paper. I could hear and feel my blood pumping through every vessel in my body; anxiety consumed me.

"Here?" I pointed to the front door, shaking on the inside. Every person walking in would see me; I'd have to speak to total strangers. I said I couldn't. Very firmly, she said, "Put this lipstick on, and all I need you to do is smile, honey." This woman taught me how to suck it up and jump in, a fundamental lesson I never forgot.

I loved work. My co-workers were all older than me and felt like family. I was earning a paycheck and started planning. There was hope.

Chapter 24

During a screaming match, Mom brought up Dad again and added details she could never take back. Not understanding the events leading up to his incarceration, I was angry with him. Whatever he did to end up in prison left me resentful. I shouted I never wanted to talk about him again. She bent down with her gown gathered and said, "He's not your dad anyway."

There have been moments in my life where I imagined things couldn't get any more fucked up. But there was always another moment. There she was, words leaving her mouth serving as Pandora's Box. The conversation and details that followed would not be resolved for me for years and left a permanent void.

She was talented at storytelling, mainly when everything revolved around her. Her story was as elaborate as a Greek tragedy about leaving my father before I was conceived, working in a diner, and never planning to go back to him. Despite her intense love for him, she couldn't deal with the abuse. That's where she met Rocco, fell madly in love with him, and got pregnant with me. Somehow, Dad persuaded her to go back to him. With baby in belly, he convinced her he'd always claim me as his child. Somehow, through this fantasy soap opera-like recollection, she'd miraculously kept his number all those years. She also knew Rocco had been looking for me. Hearing this story as a sixteen-year-old who felt like nothing was left to lose, I was hopeful again. Maybe this was it. Rocco, my real dad, would be the stable person, ready to step up and raise a child he'd never met. To a desperate sixteen-year-old, this seemed plausible.

"But you can never tell your Dad Venus. He'd kill us all."

She made one phone call, and Rocco arrived within a few days. He pulled up in a rusted hatchback. I watched this man approach the front door, frail, withered and looked like a worn-out paper bag of a person. I just wanted to get out, and he gladly did that, loaded me into his car, and drove off. He rambled about telling people he had another daughter all these years. His eyes were watery. He lived in Florida with four other children, all younger than me. About twenty minutes from Mom's house, he made his first stop to buy a tallboy beer wrapped in a brown paper bag. I watch him get completely shit-faced, driving me in a car that has no speedometer or gas gauge.

It was a nightmare, but instead, I was wide awake. I wanted to bolt up, gasping for air, and take a sip of water, and it would all be over, but this would not work out that way. I watched him guzzle beer after beer. He was a storyteller. I heard stories involving murder, drugs, and empty promises as his eyelids opened and closed slowly. The wind was hot, and my skin felt grimy from the rolled-down windows and cigarette smoke.

On our way to Florida, right outside New Orleans, he pulled over at a gas station and asked me to drive. I'd never driven on an interstate. My only experiences driving were the disastrous time I put the car in the ditch or the evening rides Glenn took me on to practice in neighborhoods. Not knowing what to do, I agreed. A small voice convinced me I could pull this off, but my gut told me differently.

As I followed the ramp back onto the interstate, he'd already passed out. I had no idea how fast I was going, whether I had gas, or where I was going. I drove. I don't remember much else until I saw a bridge. I'd never been fond of bridges. I panicked. Seeing the bridge approaching, I couldn't sort out my thoughts. I had to get out of the car immediately. I swerved to take the exit. My chest was closing; I had no choice but to get off the highway. Pulling into a gas station with a parking lot full of drunk men hanging around, I slammed on the brakes and jumped out. I shook him over and over until he finally woke up. Crying, frantic, I begged him to please wake up and drive.

When we finally arrived in Florida, he pulled into the yard of his house. I swallowed the boulder sitting in my throat. The house was not good. Not that the houses I'd lived in were great, but this was different. When he opened the door, the stench of urine slammed me in the face. There were two little kids—a boy and girl between the ages of 4 and 6—dirty, with rotten teeth. Two older kids between ten and twelve sat on the couch, one girl and one boy. It was a one-bedroom house with four kids, two adults, and now me. I remember a hole in the floor and enough roaches to carry me away. I doubted the existence of any higher power. Seven hours from home with a strange family. A family that eerily had waited for my arrival for years. None of them were surprised by my existence. Instead, they seemed to have been waiting for the call.

While in Florida, I met a friend. He and his twin sister were kind. I'm thankful for him and the friends he introduced me to. I'd hang out with them on the beach at night and during the day when I could. He took me to the most beautiful beach I'd ever seen there. We drove as far as we could, parking on the shoulder, climbed out, and hiked up huge boulders along the beach, calm and deserted. We sat there for hours. I can't recall what we talked about if anything. Above all, he never touched me. I wish him eternal happiness for that. Sitting there with him, watching waves crash against rocks, I wanted to stay forever. This was one of the few peaceful experiences I cherished. Sitting and watching the ocean's vastness away from any other human being, my mind clear. While in Florida, I escaped to the beach as often as possible.

Back at the house, Rocco and his wife often pawned items to buy a handle of vodka. When they'd run out of money, they'd pawn the Nintendo and television. It didn't matter to them as long as they got a few bucks for alcohol. On Friday, they'd scrounge together whatever money he'd earned from painting houses. Come Friday night, they'd get wasted and become violent with each other. He would remind his wife of how fat she was and how he still loved some long-lost women he hadn't seen in years. His wife would crumble and cry while the kids fought and ran around the house. Usually, they'd take off, and I'd stay with the kids. When they'd leave, I'd try to clean the house the best I could. Opening cabinets and drawers, I'd smash roach after roach. Roaches covered every surface. I chain-smoked cigarettes and killed roaches, not knowing what else to do. I lost track of the days and weeks.

Another fight started about his long-lost love, which escalated into one of their worst fights. Rocco began threatening to kill his wife and himself. I saw he had a gun. When I saw the gun, my first reaction was complete panic. Rambling and incoherent, they were both completely irrational. The kids woke up and huddled together. Rocco stood waving his gun around. Something snapped inside of me. I was raging. I'd had enough of pathetic adults and their bullshit.

"If you're going to shoot, then fucking shoot," I screamed, sickened by the situation.

I had watched them go back and forth in their pathetic verbal banter for so long that I was ready to be done with it. Rocco looked at me with his head cocked to the side and blinked several times. The kids were still huddled together. Tangled brown hair framed the faces of the little girls. His wife was drunk to the point she couldn't focus to see straight. Her eyes were swollen, pink, and puffy from crying. The view of the situation was absurd. He was a fraction of the size of a grown man—years of alcohol and poverty had chipped away at his physical presence—yet there we were, standing at his mercy behind a gun.

"Just fucking do it and be done." I meant it.

I was scared but couldn't take any of it any longer. I was screaming in his face. I wasn't just screaming at him because of his fight with his wife. I was screaming at every adult who had let me down. I wanted to be an adult so that I could do things better. I was enraged that I'd allowed myself to come that close to destruction.

At that moment, as terrified as I was, I grew even more furious and would have taken a bullet to end all the heartache. I was livid that I'd come to this, living in a house with a bunch of drunks in an unfamiliar place. I was pissed at my dad for being in prison, and I hated my mom and her husband for treating us the way they did. I should be caring for my sisters and brother in Louisiana, not here with these strangers.

Suddenly, he threw the gun and shattered the glass in the cabinet. I had called his bluff, and the show was over.

I began trying to figure out a way to get back to Louisiana. No one from my family would come and get me. My dad was still in prison. I'd met a guy before I left Louisiana. Nothing serious, but I liked him, at least what I knew of him. Desperate, I called him crying on the phone; I still have no idea what I said. Whatever it was, he was kind enough to get on the road to give me a ride back home. When I returned to Lafayette, I told my mom I never wanted to hear Rocco's name again—and I didn't until years later.

Chapter 25

When I returned to Lafayette, I went back to my job. Unfortunately, I missed a lot of school. This was a repeat of my junior year. I missed so many days that I didn't know how to catch up. Things were darker when I returned from Florida. Whatever light had been in my mother had faded. Glenn walked around like a zombie most of the time. The kids entertained themselves and took unsupervised trips around town on the city bus until the buses stopped running.

Holidays were torture. I hated watching Christmas shows on television where the entire family celebrated. There were no holiday celebrations in our house. I can remember only a couple of times we had a family meal for a holiday. Once, when asked what I wanted for Christmas, I stated that I wished to a carton of cigarettes and was given a carton of Marlboros. Another year, things were so bad I knew my mom couldn't afford to buy the kids gifts. Knowing Crystal needed shoes, I bought each kid a gift to open on Christmas Day. I also bought an expensive perfume set from the mall for my mom. I wanted to skip through holidays altogether; the expectation of happiness was too much.

During those years, it was not surprising for the cops or strangers to bring our baby brother home for being in the street in his diaper. My mom stayed locked in her room, watching soap operas, oblivious to the real world, including us.

I started dating the guy who brought me back from Florida.

One day, at Jason's house, a woman showed up to see his mother. His mother introduced us. His mother had shared my story with this woman I didn't know. She was in her early thirties and a single mom to a preschooler and toddler. She asked if I would like to live with her when I turned eighteen. I was just a few months away from eighteen and couldn't believe my ears.

Soon afterward, I broke up with Jason, but she was willing to keep the offer open. The next few months were a blur. I worked as much as I could at the mall. The people I worked with were all older; for the most part, they had their own cars and were kind enough to give me a ride to and from work. I spent lots of time at my girlfriend's apartment; she was seventeen and pregnant, living with her boyfriend downtown, not far from Mom's. There, I met JT. They were cousins, and he'd come over often to hang out. His demeanor was quiet and gentle. He was like no one I'd ever met; I wanted to be near him. He was peaceful. We started hanging out.

After work at his cousin's apartment, we'd talk for hours. I explained my situation as best I could, trying not to tell him too much, afraid he'd be overwhelmed. Mostly, the fact that I'd be moving in with a grown woman, whom I didn't know, in a week or so when I turned eighteen. Before long, we were inseparable.

On my eighteenth birthday, JT helped me move. It was much harder than I thought. I was terrified; I knew I'd never be back. If things didn't work out living with this woman, I'd have to find another way because I couldn't end up back there. All the other times, I knew I'd end up having to go back; this time was different, and I knew it was forever. That last day, while packing up, we sat on my bed. I will never forget the look on his face when Glenn blurted, "Happy Birthday" to me and tossed a joint on my bed.

As I walked out, no one in the family saw me off. No one came running to ask where I was going, and no one even had an address. To them, I was finally getting out. Now, they just needed to get Crystal out of the house. I lived with Ann for over a year. The hardest part was leaving Crystal behind. I knew if I stayed, though, I would jeopardize my future. I had to ultimately hope for the best for her.

As I left my mom's home for the last time, I prepared to enter the home of a woman I barely knew.

Chapter 26

L iving at Anne's house was depressing at first. I know that may sound inexplicable, but it was. The house was beautiful to me; it was nothing fancy but way nicer than anything I'd ever lived in. Three bedrooms, two bathrooms, a yard, air conditioning—and situated in a neighborhood directly behind the mall. Despite having everything I thought I always wanted, it wasn't my home. I was merely a guest, although she genuinely did try to make me comfortable. I worked and tried to earn my keep, constantly cleaning and helping out with her two girls. She never told me to, but I felt obligated to repay her.

As great as it was to have a decent roof over my head, I can't say it was necessarily safe. It turns out she had a mentally unstable ex-husband who was obsessed with her and stalked us. He did things like sit outside the house or at the end of the road and watch us. Once, rambling nonsense no one could understand, he entered my workplace with lit incense. I was too young to truly understand how dangerous a love-scorned, mentally ill person could be. I flicked him off when I saw him lurking. I tried to encourage her to get out and stay away from him. She told me bizarre stories about his behaviors while they were married. He put marijuana plants in the flower pot attached to the back of the mailbox to try and get us arrested. After a while, I grew to ignore his presence.

Returning from work one night, I noticed his motorcycle in our driveway. I rushed inside. She informed me he was moving back in. An invisible baseball bat struck me behind the knees. What was I going to do? For once, I wanted to be on an island where mental illness did not come to find me. I couldn't understand it; she knew he was crazy. Why would she do this? I had no options, utterly dependent on her for a place to live. Fortunately, her reconciliation plan ended as quickly as it started. But I began to seek out roommates. I didn't care how many it took; I was willing to sleep on the floor in the living room and have a place to call home. The threat of her giving in to him and bringing him into the house motivated me to get on my feet.

Despite her instabilities, she cared for me while I was there. I worked almost every night. I'd set my alarm for the following day to get up and go to school, but when it went off, I couldn't get myself out of bed to get up and dressed. I was so far behind I'd never catch up. Not to mention, I was embarrassed about being held back because of my absences. Since I'd missed so much school, I would likely be held back again during my junior year.

Sitting at her kitchen table over coffee one morning, she asked about my plan. Confused, I told her I was working that day. I was terrified she'd throw me out before I had enough money or roommates ready to move in.

"No, I mean about school, Venus. You can't keep skipping. If you want to go, you need to go. If you need a place to stay until you graduate, I don't mind you staying here. But you've got to make up your mind."

This was more than I'd ever considered about my future and school. I had no idea what to do. I didn't want to be a dropout, and I was terrified of not making something of my life and ending up like many adults I knew.

"It doesn't have to be like that. You can get your GED and go on to college. Whatever you decide, you need to stick to it. Either finish school or drop out, get your GED, and get on with your life."

The next day, I went to the front office of my high school and asked for a withdrawal form. Completely humiliated, I walked around the campus with my textbooks and withdrawal form for my teachers to sign off on. Instead of the form referencing the school I was transferring to, the secretary wrote *drop out.* I distinctly remember the track coach having to sign the form because he was my math teacher; with a wad of tobacco in his cheek, he shook his head and walked away from me. I felt worthless; he had no idea what I was going through, and it was apparent it wasn't his job. I walked up the stairs to my English class. I will never forget my teacher; despite my failure, I was in honors English. Not that I did the work to justify being in an honors course. She stepped outside to sign the form.

"Why are you doing this?"

Looking down, ashamed, I replied, "Because I have to work."

She nodded. "What is your plan?" To this day, I appreciate her asking. She cared enough to ask.

"I'm going to get my GED, go to college. Maybe be an English teacher or a writer." She didn't say much.

I left there and went directly to the GED testing site. The lady behind the desk explained I was taking a placement test to determine what remediation classes I needed before taking the GED test. I sat in a room for what seemed like hours. When I walked out, I was spent; I had never written or answered that many questions at once in my life.

Outside, I chain-smoked until she was done grading my placement test. As I walked back into the office, she looked up and asked why I had quit school. I explained because I had to work. I scored almost perfect on the writing portion and passed all other parts. I was going straight to the GED test without any remediation.

The day my class was walking down the aisle, graduating from high school, I sat at the school board, taking my GED test. I went to my best friend's house to celebrate her graduation that afternoon. Watching her in that green cap and gown was too much to take, so I left. I knew I would never be able to experience their celebration; I would forever be different. Weeks later, I received my results, saying I passed the GED and was invited to participate in the graduation ceremony.

My mom invited us back to her house after the ceremony. Once we arrived, it didn't take long for Crystal to get hit by Glenn. She ran into my old room, screaming and crying. I went in to check on her. She was hysterical like I had been so many times. Tears streaming down her face; she screamed that she hated them over and over.

My heart broke as I stood there looking at her. I turned and walked out, knowing this couldn't be the end. I just couldn't leave her alone. As I walked down my mother's front steps, Maw-maw lay on the couch, wrapped in a wool blanket, with a beanie on in the middle of May with no air conditioner. She was receiving chemo for breast cancer. Paw-paw stood at the end of the steps while Mom stood on the porch. JT was there, waiting for me to leave with him. The streetlights lit up the front porch, and on the sidewalk, we stood in the glow of the artificial light.

Paw-paw was smiling; to this day, his smile is the most genuine smile I've ever seen. "Well, now, what are you going to do?"

Proud and serious, I said, "I'm going to college."

"College," he said, pulling his head back, "Why don't you do something with your looks?" I put my head down and focused on the sidewalk. I was ashamed. Ashamed, that's all my family saw in me. No one in my family had ever gone to college. I felt like going to college was too good for me. My mom walked towards me.

"Why don't you just get married and have a baby?" Turning and walking away was all I could think to do. They honestly thought those things would be best for my future. No one in our family had ever done anything other than struggle. I had to be different. Getting there would be a different story.

THIS IS NOT FOR YOU

Part 2

Chapter 27

I walked into the bar, my chest tight and body tense, holding my breath, preparing the best I could to face my mother over lunch in public. I can hardly tolerate how she speaks to wait staff like they are servants. As I made my way around the corner, my eyes dart frantically, trying to locate her at the table. I wanted to be sure to sit away from her at the table. Being near her makes me too anxious; I instantly become defensive. It is only my sisters I see; they sense my anxiety and laugh out loud.

"She's not here." Rose chuckles, taking a sip of her drink. "Why'd ya'll think I'd invite her to lunch? I'm not that cruel. Crystal did the same thing." Rose shakes her head back and forth, grinning.

Confused, I pulled out my chair and sat at the high table, still trying to figure out what was happening. I thought for sure Rose would have Mom along to look for her wedding dress.

"I'll take a large margarita with sangria," I tell the waitress over my shoulder. Rose orders a shot. Funny how my apprehension lifted like a fog during a morning drive. We begin to fill each other in on the latest bizarre occurrences from Mom and Glenn. Rose lived through struggles different from Crystal and I—mainly because her father adored her. But our mother played no favorites when it came to cursing out her children and letting us know how we inconvenienced her. We started the lunch by asking if anyone had heard from Mom. Oddly enough, at that time, Crystal, in her thirties, communicated with our mother regularly. Rose keeps in touch by default when she visits or contacts her dad. On the other hand, I could only bring myself to speak to Mom on rare occasions.

"V, you really should talk to her." Crystal is trying to push my buttons.

"No, I really shouldn't. I have nothing to say." I reached for my glass and took a long sip of the margarita, which instantly gave me a head freeze. I do not distance myself because I am angry. I am indifferent; I have moved on; nothing is left to share with her, and she depleted me. On the rare occasion when I spoke to her, I felt removed as Mom tried to talk about the realities of her world on the phone.

My sisters and I are together to look for wedding dresses. Rose was getting married in the fall. I change the subject, asking about the wedding. Immediately, Crystal reminds us of what happened at my wedding years ago. It's not that we dwell on our childhood; it's more like we won't let each other forget, which allows us to always be prepared for what's next.

"What?" Rose questions. She was still in middle school when JT and I got married.

"You don't remember what Mom did?" Crystal laughs as she shakes her head and grabs a chip.

"Mom threw up." Cut the crap and get to the point— that's always been my style.

"What? Why don't I know these things?" She lifts her palms in the air before grabbing her shot.

"She hadn't seen V's dad in forever, so she got drunk." Crystal talks while her mouth is full of chips and salsa.

"She drank too much wine. I was talking to a friend when someone came out of the bathroom and said there's a lady on the floor, throwing up, in the bathroom." I looked at Rose, watching her reaction, and continued. "I knew it was her without anyone having to tell me. I went in and helped her off the floor. I walked her out of my wedding. Your dad took her home."

We all drank more than we ate during lunch. Being around my sisters always brings me back to the long road it took before we could sit around and make light of our past. Maybe it was our age differences, but I felt strained when we were together for a long time. Like I should have fixed things for all of us, and the fact that I hadn't left me feeling empty.

Working in the mall, I eventually found two roommates, and we moved into a two-bedroom apartment. I begged the clothing store manager for as many hours as I could get. I spent so much time there that the store felt like home. Despite the hours I put in, I was still short on cash most of the time. I often counted change to buy something to eat in the Food Court.

In the apartment, we each had our own space. I slept on the floor on my side of the room. I didn't have a bed, but it never occurred to me I needed one. Eventually, as friends came by to visit, they'd bring hand-me-down furniture donations or odds and ends from their parents. Things were good enough for me.

Several years before leaving home, I was aware of the progression of Glenn's drug problem. He was rarely awake and sweated profusely when he was. He'd disappear for long periods. My mother's verbal tirades were constant when I finally moved out. Crystal had no one to look after her once I left the house.

I remember the strange feeling I had one afternoon when my mother called to let me know Glenn had finally entered rehab. Doctors were not sure he would survive the detox stage. In his early thirties, his heart was weakened by the amount of drugs he shot up regularly. My mother was not compassionate about his risk of dying during this process. She was angry at being inconvenienced by the medical bills, chanting over and over again how could he do this to her? Not his children or himself. Once again, she was the victim. Without him, how would she get to and from the grocery store? Not ever learning how to drive, she could not cope with the idea of not having him around. Her anger focused on Crystal as well. Somehow, this was Crystal's fault, a child under the age of ten. She vented in circles about how Crystal tormented the other two, Rose and David, their children together.

When I answered the phone, she screamed into the receiver that Crystal was evil, and Glenn wanted her out. These conversations shattered my insides. I knew the situation was helpless. I rarely spoke about my Mom or my family to my roommates. I did not know where to begin the story. I just hoped it would get better for Crystal's sake.

Glenn survived his first stay in rehab but not without surgery. He needed a pacemaker. I continued to pick up extra hours at the mall to make ends meet. My other roommates had parents to fall back on; I did not have that luxury. Shortly after we moved into our apartment, JT began staying with us. Michelle helped me budget and keep my limited finances straight. Michelle, who enrolled at the University of Southern Louisiana, USL, had recently quit working in the mall and got an office job, which paid more and had great hours. I was envious. We'd lay around, and I'd tell her how I wanted to go to college but thought it couldn't happen. Looking back, I am forever grateful for those long conversations. Michelle would lay it all out for me. She instructed me to go to USL and fill out a financial aid application. I said I would but was deathly afraid of what that meant, so I avoided it. One day, I was sprawled across Michelle's twin-sized bed—she tossed off her backpack and handed me a document, a financial aid application. She explained the wording step by step. Together, we completed the application. I'm unsure if I would have attempted to fill it out otherwise. That one document would eventually change everything for me.

Chapter 28

I was sitting on the floor in the living room of our apartment, the day my plans began to change without me knowing. I had the cordless phone cradled in the crook of my neck and shoulder. I was tossing a rag doll filled with catnip at our cate. My mom was ranting about Crystal being a fucking little bitch: Glenn wanted her out of the house, he made it clear it was either my sister or him. Through her shouts and panted breaths, she told me she would not allow Crystal to ruin her marriage. I was accustomed to hearing these accusations. From as far back as I can remember, growing up, we were always cursed at me, the whore, slut, and bitch; Crystal was always the evil bitch. Now that I was out, I separated myself from this past and tried desperately to have some type of relationship with my mother; when she called, I listened absently. I was not ready for what was about to follow.

"We are bringing her to her father."

That statement silenced our conversation. I couldn't breathe as my neck began pulsating. My throat felt bruised as I tried to swallow. I could hear Mom breathing through her nose into the receiver, waiting for my reaction. I'd been thrown out of her house during my adolescence but always returned once I ran out of places to stay. Crystal had been hospitalized over my mother's irrational accusations of her being evil. This was different. A hopelessness filled me. Crystal had not seen her father since preschool. He lived in Pennsylvania and had no true home of his own. He was a truck driver, a gypsy. I knew I might never hear from her again. I began pleading, trying to determine if my mom was exaggerating. Certainly, they wouldn't drive halfway across the country.

"Please, Mom, don't."

I knew Crystal's dad was an alcoholic. The last thing I wanted was for my sister to be tossed to a practical stranger in an unfamiliar place. I offered for her to spend a few days at my apartment. The conversation ended as my mother and I screamed at each other.

JT walked out of the back of our apartment as I began to break down. I couldn't explain the cruelness of the conversation. Even if I could, he couldn't understand its magnitude. His family was nothing like mine. He tried to console me, saying Mom was probably angry and wouldn't do it. I knew them better, and that's exactly what they did. Together she and Glenn loaded up my sister, and he drove her to Pennsylvania. She was left on the doorsteps of her dad's cousin, a stranger. I tried to get information about how she was doing from Mom, but she didn't even know where Crystal was for a while.

Chapter 29

Michelle and I decided to move out of the apartment and into a house. We wanted a yard and more space. Looking in the newspaper, we found a two-bedroom house that fit our budget. Although I wasn't familiar with the neighborhood, it seemed good enough for us. We were young and eager to move, so we paid the deposit.

The location was in an area of high crime. One night, a few girls came over to watch movies. There was a commotion outside. When we went out to see what was going on, we saw a brick had been thrown through the driver's window and everything stolen out of the car. I called 911; the police arrived and wouldn't even take a report. The advice he gave was not to lock our car doors; they will only break your windows. We spent many evenings watching the chaos of crime surrounding us.

Michelle was in school; for the most part, we all worked as much as possible and hung out on the porch when we were off. We drank beer from brown paper bags while watching criminals work the streets. After being in Pennsylvania for a while, my sister shuffled between her dad's distant relatives and friends. eventually, a family friend took her in, and she seemed to be doing better until she started acting out. they got sick of dealing with her, and she was returned to my mom's. it had been a while since she was home, and my mom didn't seem angry that Crystal was going back. Since Glenn was off of the hard stuff, things would smooth over. Hopefully, Crystal realized my mom and Glenn were serious and that she would lay low. Don't fight back as much.

The Ford LTD I was driving was breaking leaving me stranded regularly. Our good friend Andrew taught me how to clean the carburetor to get it started. I was adding at least a quart of oil a day. I needed money or credit to buy new transportation. Michelle helped me get a job at the same office she worked, but I was in sales and had completely different hours than she did. I desperately needed a car to get to and from work. JT asked his dad to help me, and he paid to repair my vehicle. I was embarrassed. I hated asking anyone for help, but I was grateful. It worked for a while, but it just kept breaking down. Michelle co-signed a loan for me to buy a new used vehicle. Not only did it start every time I turned the key, but it had air conditioning. I am eternally grateful to her.

College was another story. I mailed in the financial aid application but was denied eligibility because the government thought a person couldn't file for independent status, making the low annual income I was making. I was devastated. The financial aid office wouldn't approve any college funding, including student loans. I resorted to the idea that I would just have to work. I was sitting at our kitchen table when my mom called. Crystal was back; we had recently found her at an older boys' house that wasn't in school anymore. Mom suspected Glenn was using again and that he was going to leave her if Crystal stayed. Mom tried to convince me Crystal deserved to be put in a girl's home.

"Venus, she punched Glen in the heart. She's trying to kill him." I was confused and didn't understand why she was telling me this. There was nowhere for Crystal to go. Her dad sent her back.

"Mom, she's your daughter. You can't just get rid of her."

That's when she said something I will never forget. Despite everything, until this point in my life, I still felt the need to communicate with her and have some type of relationship with her. Many years ago, this conversation began to close off something profound inside: the hope I had to have a relationship with my mother. No matter what she had put us through, nothing compared to hearing my mother say she was going to abandon

Crystal to the state.

"What? What are you talking about?" I was trying to keep my emotions under control.

" I've already looked into it. You can bring your child to the courthouse here in New Iberia on Tuesdays and give them to the State. Kids that are out of control. I can't handle her anymore." Her voice was rising, and my chest was getting tight.

"Mom, think about what you were saying. They are going to put her in a girls' home. Do you understand what that means?"

I wanted her to be rational praying she would reconsider. My sister would be with strangers. Around kids who would expose her to things that would only influence her in a way I didn't even want to imagine. I pictured my sister in a room full of girls while Rose and David were at home, in their home. It was the week before Thanksgiving break. I begged her to let Crystal come and stay with Michelle, JT, and me for the week. I offered to pick her up from school.

"What the fuck do you want me to do? I'm not losing my husband. You fucking understand me. She punched him in the chest. She tried to kill him."

"She didn't try to kill him. He hit her, and she hit him back. Mom!" I lost it, screaming. Together, we screamed until I hung up. Not knowing how to approach me, JT came into the room. He knew bits and pieces, but I'd never explained the entire story. Until that day, I didn't know where to begin, but somehow I did. Sitting on the couch in our living room, I cried as the words describing my childhood somehow found their way out of my mouth. He eventually got up and handed me a phone book. Confused, I looked at him, not knowing what he wanted.

"Call someone. there has to be someone who can help your sister." I was even more confused. Help? Who could possibly help? For 19 years, it was only me, the only one who could help, and I hadn't done a very good job of it. He opened the cover of the phone book and pointed to a 1-800-abuse hotline. For some reason, this terrified me. Here I was, desperate to save my sister, but I was terrified of what would happen to my mom. After all these years, something inside me wanted to protect our mom, but at that moment, I had to choose, and I chose my sister. If no one was willing to help her, I had to.

When the woman answered the hotline, I rattled our entire life story. I doubt she could understand anything I was saying between my sobs. That day, I opened the door to something deep inside of me. Nothing could contain it. Eventually, she stopped me mid-sentence, explaining that she was only the receptionist and needed to get someone on the line to assist. I began again with that person, and she never interrupted me. Eventually, she asked what schools the kids attended. She said she was sending social workers to the schools. The woman assured me everything would be okay. She would call me back.

While I waited, my mom called, warning me if I tried to pick up my sister from school, they would have me arrested. They wanted her gone, and if she stayed with me during the break, I would only bring her back. Mom was clear that she wanted her out of the house for good. I cursed and screamed at her before hanging up the phone. JT honestly had no idea what to do with me. I don't remember how he talked me into it, but I ended up in his parents' living room that day, telling the entire story. I wanted to take Crystal. I was exhausted. I had no idea how I would support her, but I would figure it out.

Chapter 30

That night, a social worker called. She started the conversation by saying I'm not supposed to tell you this. She described her visit with my mother. She and Glenn denied everything and made Crystal out to be a juvenile delinquent. The social worker knew it was a show; she would try her best to help me. She then told me when my mom was planning on going to the courthouse to abandon my sister. That is what I wasn't supposed to know. The social worker said she would be there for the Office of Community Services. If I were there, I could tell the judge I wanted Crystal. She reminded me I was only 19 and the judge might not grant me guardianship because of my age. The social worker also explained there was no better place for the state to put my sister than with me. If they refused to let her come with me, she would be tossed from foster homes to girls' homes. She was already in middle school, and there just weren't any adoptive parents wanting to take in teenagers. I knew Crystal would act out even more in this environment.

I told Maggie, JT's mom, the date and time I would go to the courthouse. She told me she wanted to be there as well. I tried to talk her out of it. I knew how bad it would be. I was well aware of what my mother was capable of. Maggie wouldn't hear of it, and the morning I was to come face to face with my mother, Maggie picked me up.

I was sick to my stomach. I knew Mom would lose control and

scream at me in front of every person there. The night before, I couldn't sleep and cried the entire night. I felt like a traitor facing my mother the way I was about to. Even though I knew what she and Glenn were doing was wrong. I didn't want to hurt her. I suppose that is a natural innate instinct, wanting to stick by your parents. But what choice do you have when faced with the reality that your parents don't try to protect you? I was even more terrified of what would happen to Crystal, imagining how my mom and Glenn would react when they saw me. My chest felt as if it were going to explode at any moment. The social worker had already told me the entire purpose of child protective services was reunifying the family. They would want Mom and Glenn to go to counseling. Mom made it very clear when the social worker visited her that she did not want Crystal and refused counseling services. She also did not want people from the "state" in her home.

I walked into the building light headed and with tunnel vision. The rapidness of my pulse causing a thudding noise in my ears. Outside the room was a line of adults and children. The social worker explained Tuesday was Family Court Day. Parents charged with abuse or neglect went before the judge, along with families who wanted to relinquish their parental rights. Our mom was the only parent there to give up her child. The other families were there to try and get their children back.

I followed the social worker to the front of the room to sit. I sat between the social worker and Maggie. I can't recall ever being that petrified in my entire life. I couldn't stop my body from trembling. I saw my mom walk in before she saw me. She and Glenn sat while I watched. Crystal eventually made eye contact with me. She bolted from them to me. I remember the confused look on Mom's face. She didn't understand. I saw the moment it clicked. I could see it on her face. Her expression refocused, and she realized she was looking at me, her daughter. She had no idea who Maggie was. She had never met Maggie. Crystal wrapped her arms around my neck. I couldn't take my eyes off of my mom. I couldn't understand how a mother could do this to her children.

"Am I going home with you?" She asked directly in my ear.

Tears began to roll down my face. I couldn't lie and didn't want to get her hopes up. I squeezed her tightly into my grip. I had no idea of how any of this would turn out.

"I don't know. I'm going to try real hard, though."

Maggie sat still as she looked back at my mother. Crystal refused to leave my side. I remember asking the social worker if it was okay for Crystal to sit with us. She said yes, either way Mom and Glenn wouldn't leave with her.

Someone entered and said the court would be starting, and everyone needed to wait in the hall for our names to be called. We began filing into the waiting area. My mom purposely stayed in her seat until I walked by. As I did, she jolted up, gripping her purse and walked next to me.

"You fucking little bitch. What do you think you are doing? They're not going to give her to you. If they do, they will only want me to take her back when she eventually starts acting up again. How can you do this to me?" I could feel her breath as the words filled the air.

I knew things were only going to escalate. I refused to look at her. As I tried to ignore her, my heart pounded. I was lightheaded and trembling. I kept walking, looking straight ahead, while Crystal held my hand. Maggie was behind us with the social worker. Glenn walked ahead of us, his head hanging down.

The hall was packed with people. I retreated as far away from everyone as I possibly could. Someone in a uniform went to Mom and told her she needed to lower her voice. Maggie and I sat in silence. Mom obeyed the orders briefly but quickly started shouting at us again from across the hall. I looked around and saw other mothers who had charges of neglect and abuse against their children, staring at my mom and whispering. I was exhausted wanting to fold over and disappear. Desperately wanting peace. My eyes were swollen from the constant stream of tears. I felt weak. I just wanted her to shut up. We sat in the hall for hours, waiting for our names to be called. Eventually, Glenn took her outside, which gave us a short silence from her constant verbal assaults. I had no idea how I would have the energy to explain everything before the judge.

When Glenn and my mom returned, her insults immediately started again. I went to Glenn and told him to shut her up, or I would have her arrested for harassment. I walked into the bathroom. I stood at the sink, splashing water on my face. As I picked up my head, my mother stood behind me. The bathroom was cold and bright. The brightness made me squint. My eyes burned from tears.

"What the fuck are you doing, Venus? She's my daughter, and if I want to give her up, I can. You can't take care of her."

Maggie came into the bathroom, standing at the door. "Leave her alone."

My mother turned around. " Who are you? Let me guess. I bet Venus never told you how she used to sneak out to meet boys and sleep at their houses at night. She's a fucking whore, you hear me?"

I was beyond humiliated that Maggie had to endure this. I knew she wouldn't believe my mother's words, but it still crushed me she was hearing them.

"Let me ask you something. Where were you when your daughter was sneaking out? Where was her mother?" Maggie told me to sit in the hall. When I walked past my mother, she began to follow me. I went to the security guard and pointed at her. I told him if he saw her approach me again, I wanted her arrested. He walked over and explained to my mom and Glenn what would happen if she continued to harass me.

Shortly afterward, our names were called. Mom and Glenn walked in before us. A woman who was there for charges against her child stopped my mom.

"Honey, I ain't no saint to be standing here in this courthouse with my own child." Her hair was set tall on top of her head, and her nails were bright blue, long and curved. She was a big woman with tight clothes and excessive makeup. "But I'll tell you one thing: You the devil talking to your daughter like that." My mother continued to walk past her as if she had never heard the woman.

Behind the closed doors, a table was surrounded by adults: several from child protective services, a judge, and others who could have been from anywhere I would have never known. We were told to sit while Maggie had to wait outside in the hall. I don't remember who started to speak first, but Mom started screaming immediately. Every adult at the table seemed to be caught off guard and startled by the way their bodies jumped. She was warned numerous times before the judge had to have her removed. Now Crystal and I sat with only Glenn and the remaining strange adults at the table. I sat silently as he attempted to explained why she was being abandoned. Tears streamed down my face while my chest heaved short, shallow breaths. Eventually, the judge asked why I was there. I explained I wanted my sister to live with me. He asked me how old I was. I told him I was 19. Without any hesitation, he said she could not come with me. I was sobbing. I then began frantically explaining the years of abuse and what Crystal and I had endured. I told the panel about my mom being in jail for dealing. Glenn was an addict and abused Crystal. I sobbed between every word. The adults sat speechless until one man looked at me and said, " Honey, your tears won't get you sympathy from us."

I was appalled. A switch flipped. I got hot and wanted to start screaming profanities like my Mom, but knew better. How could he think I was trying to get sympathy? What good would sympathy do for us? I only wanted my sister. A woman farther down the table from him leaned forward and said, " I truly don't think this young lady cares if you sympathize with her."

Glenn tried to intervene, but I immediately told them to check my mother's arrest record. I had a clean record and would do anything they told me to if allowed to take my sister to my home. The social worker pointed out to the judge that being with a relative was better than putting Crystal in a group home.

Every adult at the table agreed Crystal would not be returning with Mom and Glenn, but where should she go? Still undecided. Glenn was told to wait in the hall. Once he walked out, the adults pelted me with questions. Where did I work? How many people lived in the house? Who would be there when my sister got home from school everyday? Eventually, the judge said I would have frequent visits from the social workers. I was only allowed to take her because she had nowhere else to go. I agreed to every requirement. The judge explained that the goal would be the reunification of the family. I knew my mother would never cooperate with them, but I was happy enough that Crystal would be coming home with me. In time, they would see my mom would never do what was expected for reunification, but that was not my battle that day. For the moment I had won. Crystal would be cared for by me.

Chapter 31

L ooking back, I thought that the day I faced my mother in court to take Crystal would be the hardest I'd have to face. Quickly, I discovered there would be many more days that would be just as intense. I am grateful I had no idea how difficult the journey would be. I wasn't prepared to successfully help Crystal cope with the damage done to her. She was hurt and did not exactly welcome my efforts. JT and I transformed our small living room into our bedroom and gave Crystal our old room for her privacy. She stayed in her room most of the time. I tried to get her to come out by coaxing her with cheap gifts and snacks but would fail. I couldn't understand.

A feeling of dread began to fill me. I was torn with guilt, what was I doing wrong. Instantly, I knew things would be forever different for me. I took on the unbelievable responsibility of raising my sister. I couldn't just pick up and hang out with friends like I once had. The realization that I had suddenly become a parent overnight hit me in a way that removed my carefree spirit. I imagined it would only be a matter of time before JT took off to get on with his life.

A few days after moving in with us, I took Crystal to the mall for a haircut. Her thick, frizzy hair hadn't been cut as long as she could remember. This might help her escape her shell. She didn't speak the entire way to the mall. She just stared out the window. I didn't know what to say either. When we arrived, she sat down, and the lady asked how she wanted her haircut. Crystal just sat there and stared at her. I tried to get her to talk, but she wouldn't. I was frustrated. I couldn't understand. Not only had she been through so much for her age, but she was also a teenager. I was not equipped, being 19 years old, to understand the complexities she was dealing with. This often caused me to overreact when the best thing I could have done was just let her be. Our relationship quickly became very complicated.

I remember thinking, why did she have to make this harder than it already was? I expected her to instantly be happy and comfortable. In hindsight, that was far from possible. I finally told the lady to cut it to make it look better. She sprayed her hair with a water bottle, gathered the top, twisted it, and secured it with a hair clip. I watched her take the comb and drag it through her hair once. The woman stopped, stared for a minute, and then stepped back. She made a gesture with her hand for me to walk over. As I approached, she pointed to my sister's head. It was infested with lice. I stood and stared down. I could see lice the size of ticks jumping off of my sister's head; they were everywhere. That night, I began treating her, removing them one by one. Accepting the silence that came along with the moment.

JT and I began looking for our own place. I told him more than once to move out on his own. I'd rather him leave sooner than later. I knew this was a burden he should not have to share. He refused, always assuring me he wanted to be there. His dad suggested we buy a trailer instead of renting. This was too much for me to think about with everything else on my mind. Before I knew it, we were living in a two-bedroom trailer. His dad helped us buy it. The trailer park was small, with only a horseshoe set up. It was perfect for us. Maggie wrote the governor of Louisiana a letter on my behalf, questioning why I could not qualify for student loans. Within months, I was enrolled at USL, majoring in English, and going to school on student loans.

Crystal started making friends in middle school, and things were moving along. We were required to attend monthly family meetings at the Louisiana Department of Children and Families

Services office in New Iberia. Once a month, I had to miss work and take Crystal out of school to attend. The goal was to visit with our mom and Glenn to begin the reunification process. Additionally, Crystal started to attend counseling.

Each time, we had to sit and wait at the DCFS office. Mom and Glenn never once showed up. At first, the social workers tried rescheduling, reassuring us they would show up next time. We knew better. Finally, my mom told the social worker to stop scheduling the meetings she refused to attend. The director in charge told me he'd never encountered a situation like this before, his voice sounded nervous. Each time we showed up, and she didn't, I wasn't surprised, but they were. What I found devastating was that the social workers didn't see how hurtful this was to Crystal. She was reminded each month that our mother didn't want her. After months The State of Louisiana finally acknowledged that reunification was not a realistic goal for Crystal.

JT and I were then required to attend weekly training to become certified foster parents. At first, I was reluctant to tell him. What 20-year-old wanted to participate in parenting classes for foster parents? He never complained, nor did he ever miss a class. During this time, social workers visited our home regularly and our jobs. They went to Crystal's school to meet with her teachers, which mortified her.

Chapter 32

I did everything I could to comply with the social workers' demands. On the other hand, Crystal didn't make things easy for us. Once she entered high school, like most teens she became rebellious. I became extremely overprotective, terrified that if she got in trouble, they would pull her out of my home. Crystal and I became forces pulling in opposite directions, neither of us willing to give in.

During this time, we were completely broke. JT was working part-time and taking classes at a technical college while I had to withdraw from college to work full-time. We were simply trying to make ends meet. I noticed Crystal sneaking out at night and tried to keep her in, but the more I tried to keep her out of trouble, the more she rebelled. I found myself becoming frustrated over the simplest things I caught her doing. Our relationship was strained, our roles confused. No longer was I a sister but rule enforcer, disciplinarian. She pulled away as I acted more like a mother and less like a sister. Looking back, I realize I was trying to control something I had no power over. I was trying to fix her. I couldn't erase the things that had happened to her, and I shouldn't have attempted to. My need to pretend that we could pick up and act like our prior lives didn't exist more about healing myself. All she wanted was for me to be her sister.

One night, as I pulled up to the trailer, I saw her sitting on the wooden steps, looking thinner than ever, smoking a cigarette. She hardly ate, despite my efforts to cook for her. As my headlights focused on her, I noticed that something was different - she had shaved her head completely bald. I was furious, but I knew that arguing about it wouldn't change anything. I took her acts of rebellion as personal attacks, wondering why she couldn't just be happy.

When Crystal turned 16, she started working. I would bring her back and forth to work, and eventually, I was able to save enough money to buy her a used car. JT was working offshore, and Crystal was coming home less and less. I set curfews for her, but she wouldn't come home on time. Soon, she had the option to stay in foster care with us under the state's guidelines or file for independence from the state, giving me legal rights to her. She was tired of the meetings, and both of us were weary of the social workers constant presence. I should have known how quickly things would change once she was no longer a foster child. With me working full-time and JT working offshore, we finally had enough money to treat ourselves to things like eating out or grabbing a beer at a bar. It was nice when JT was home, but when he was away, I felt lost. I no longer had contact with most of my friends. I let caring for my sister consume me. When JT left for work, my sole responsibility was watching over my teenage sister too closely.

I'd sit alone for hours, worrying about where she was or what could happen to her. When she finally came home, I'd pelt her with questions, growing furious with her lack of answers, I would start to argue. Her friends often asked to come hang out but quickly changed their minds once they realized I didn't act like a sister. I started spending time with a couple of my girlfriends who moved downtown. When I was with them, I could forget about my responsibility for a while and enjoy the light-headedness of drinks.

It didn't take long for me to grow bored with the monetary reward of working for a corporation at such a young age. I felt desperate when I thought of my future, doing a job that had absolutely no importance to me for the rest of my life. I wanted to do something I loved. JT grew tired of being away from home just to make money. We quit our jobs in the same week without really talking about it. I re-enrolled in college, and he began trying to figure out what he wanted to do. I went to school in the mornings and worked part-time in the evenings. Crystal was no longer considered a foster child but independent from the state.

I obtained an office job for an oilfield supply company doing accounting and receptionist work. There have been times when I have been blessed without any knowledge or recognition of the importance of what was happening to me. The owner inspired me beyond words. Although I did not have the stability of my parents, I sought out parent-like figures like the owner and his wife. He allowed me to work a steady job while having the freedom to schedule my courses as the university offered them. He knew the importance of completing my education and looked over me, giving me the encouragement I needed to see my education through. I worked for him for years until I finally finished my first degree. I often wonder if I would have completed that first degree without small opportunities like the one he gave me.

While working and studying, I still had to balance caring for Crystal. JT and I sat at a college bar within walking distance from our trailer one night. It was our home away from home. We sat around with old friends from high school and played foosball and shot pool, joined by a few friends we walked home. While the rest went to the backyard, I stopped to use Crystal's bathroom. She and a friend were hanging out at a coffee shop. I noticed the note folded on the counter. I opened it. As I scanned the note, I realized she'd used the cash I gave her earlier to buy acid. I panicked at the thought of what would be next for her. Crystal had been through so much I was afraid she would begin experimenting with other drugs that could leave her addicted.

There's no way to explain it other than I was irrational after finding the note. I bolted out the trailer and got into my car. I drove recklessly into the parking lot of the coffee shop like a lunatic. I wanted to scare her, but what I did next could have gotten us both killed. As she and her girlfriend got in the car, I don't remember whether I said anything. I was beyond pissed. I desperately wanted her to have a future, and every time she did something wrong, I felt like she was blowing her chance. I would not let her throw it all away. I drove with a vengeance, weaving through traffic and speeding through red lights. I barely stopped the car before her friend jumped out when I pulled into her driveway.

I wanted to teach Crystal a lesson, and together that night, we learned exactly how irrational I was. We lived in an area that could go from college life to dark dead-end roads filled crime with one wrong turn. I thought driving down one of those dark roads would give her a taste of reality. As I turned down the road in my maroon hatchback, what those men saw were two young females who either wanted something from them or maybe thought we were willing to give them something.

As I drove down the dead-end road, it seemed as if people knew we were in the wrong place. At first, there were a handful of people on the street. When I drove further down to find a place to turn around, more people came off the porches and out of the houses. Crystal was scared. I was terrified. I pulled into a yard to turn around. As I focused on the road ahead, the street began to be lined with people. I was trembling, my palms sweating, not knowing what would happen the closer we got to the crowd. I can't say for sure, but somehow, I remember feeling like the men were laughing. One guy reached out for Crystal's door as if to try to open it.

"Roll up the fucking windows. Lock your door!"

Crystal was screaming, not words just sounds. We were both freaking out. I didn't understand exactly what she was saying until I looked straight ahead. A man was standing in the middle of the road, waiting for us. There was no way around him. I gripped the steering wheel with both hands. I smashed the accelerator to the ground. I had no idea what would happen next, but there was no way I was giving up and sitting there, waiting for them to get us. The car jumped forward, accelerating too fast. I couldn't tell if they were still trying to reach the doors. All I could focus on was the man in the middle of the road, gesturing for me to go towards him. Taunting me. He got closer and closer; my headlights had to be blinding him. A crowd was forming around us.

"You're going to fucking hit him!" I could barely understand what Crystal was screaming as she sobbed. I do clearly remember knowing I was willing to hit him if I had to.

"It's either him or us, and I'm not fucking dying."

I meant it, and Crystal knew it. Right before my car would have hit him, he jumped out of the way. I ran the stop sign and took a left onto the street I should have never turned on in the first place. That night Crystal only learned I was a little more irrational than she thought. I knew my tactics didn't help her from experimenting with drugs, but she did do a better job at hiding them for me. I am still grateful the man jumped out of the way that night; knowing I would have hit him if I had to is one thing. Living with having done it, would have been a different story.

I wish things turned out in the end the way I planned. Crystal wanted to do things her way. I refused to sit back and let her come and go as she pleased. She had a new friend with whom she spent most of her time. I decided to give her an ultimatum: either come home when I say or give me the house key and be on your own. Not surprisingly, she turned in her house key. I honestly thought she'd get it together and come home. She didn't. I wanted her life to get easier; instead, I knew her struggles were just starting.

Somehow, through this, I stayed in contact with our mom. Shortly after graduating from college, I noticed Glenn was acting strange. Before long, I realized he was using more than ever. For a short time, he and my mother would stop by and visit with JT and me at our new house.

Eventually, Crystal moved back in with us along with her 1-year-old daughter until she could get on her feet. When Glenn and Mom visited us, Glenn would nod out while sitting in the living room. Mom never apologized, much less acknowledged what we went through that day in court or how she was able to turn her back on us, allowing me to struggle to raise her daughter for years. When Glenn was awake, he would ramble about things that made no sense half the time. Sweating and pale he'd take gulps of his bourbon and coke when he came to from nodding off.

Mom pretended not to notice he was using again. Things were as normal as they could be for us.

Soon after Crystal moved out again JT and I were expecting our first child. Things were calm for a change. Until Mom called and said, Glenn was back in rehab. She claimed she was completely oblivious to the fact that he had started using again. I called her on it. The track marks were visible and Glenn put zero effort into trying to hide them. How could she not know? She attacked me, demanding how could I know and not tell her. Once again she found a way to blame me.

That day in court so long ago was the angriest I had ever seen my mother. When Glenn went back into rehab, that anger returned and lived within her. Rage consumed her to the point that I could no longer stomach.

Chapter 33

After I gave birth, my perspective on my past changed. Looking at my son, I realized how much I longed for my parents and wanted to have a nurturing relationship with them. I could never imagine not being there for my own children. I vowed to never let my children feel the pain I felt by my parents. My father reentered my life again and became a very important person to my son and, later, my first daughter. My father and I reconnected deeply for the first three years of my son's life. The relationship was everything I'd ever hoped for, just being able to reach out and connect regularly. I looked forward to his visits and phone calls. My dad was kind and loved with all of himself. His embrace was like home. He made me feel irreplaceable. My children adored him, and he treated them like royalty.

I began my career in education, teaching predominantly at-risk students. Connecting with students came naturally to me.

My mother and I became more distant. Anytime I spoke to her, she would bring up Glenn's drug use. The more she ranted about how he could have done this to her, the angrier I became. What about what was done to us, my sister and me? After being called names like bitch or whore my entire life, watching her side with her husband over us, her children, I couldn't ignore the feelings I had pulling at me as a new mother. Eventually, I stopped answering her calls.

Nothing would change her. Our communication became

distant, and we saw each other only a handful of times a year. My dad, on the other hand, began to pull away from me and my family, leaving me to explain the vanishing act to my children.

Around this time, Paw-paw and I would visit often. He was so proud of how I had turned out, having my own home and being a college graduate and teacher. We'd sit and drink cold beer together as often as I could. I loved the sound of his deep and warm voice. He'd me at work,

" V, it's Paw-paw. Meet me at Texas Roadhouse by 5:30 p.m."

There would be no debate, no matter what I had previously planned. I would rearrange my schedule to meet his request. No special occasion, when he set his mind to something there was no changing it. I remember the day he came by to say the military would start paying him a disability check for his hearing loss from the Foreign Wars he had fought in. He would finally have the financial stability he had earned. For a few years, he and Maw-maw traveled a little. He would treat us all to dinner at a local seafood restaurant, something we had never had the luxury of doing while I was growing up.

One afternoon, he showed up at my house with a freezer chest full of meat and an ice chest packed with beer. We stood at my kitchen counter while we talked and laughed together over cold Coors Light. I wish I could remember those conversations, but the details aren't important; the laughter is what I want to remember forever.

When he first started complaining of stomach problems, I blew it off, thinking it would pass. After several weeks, the complaints continued. I became more concerned when we got together for dinner, and he didn't order a beer. The doctor said it was Crohn's disease. After taking the prescribed medicine, he got worse. Sitting across from me at his kitchen table, he confided in me that he was suffering. The pain was evident in his eyes. For him to reveal he was suffering meant I would soon face my worst fear: losing him. I begged him to go to the hospital, but he refused. To him, the doctor knew best, he was concerned the VA wouldn't cover the charges if he went to a regular hospital. The VA doctor diagnosed him with Crohn's, and he was not about to challenge what the doctor said.

We planned a birthday dinner for him at his favorite restaurant. It had only been a few weeks since I'd last seen him. As I approached him in the parking lot the site of him startled me. His gaunt figure caught me off guard, I knew I was staring but couldn't look away. He still managed to laugh that night and ordered a dinner he wouldn't usually order. Which he certainly did not attempt to eat. I sat helpless, wanting to fix him as I felt the air being pulled from my body.

By the time he did go to the hospital he couldn't bare the pain any longer, the doctor's operated and saw advanced colon cancer, which had progressed so far they knew he'd never make it out of the hospital. I was sitting in his hospital room when the doctor came in with the news.

"Well, what's it look like?" Paw-paw asked.

The doctor went on to say he had stage four colon cancer. Lots of other medical terms slipped out of the doctor's mouth, but I lost focus. My skin hot and damp as the words hung in the air. My body felt as if it were floating above my chair wanting to grab those words and put them all back where they came from.

"Well, four isn't that bad, right? How many stages are there?" He was confident.

My chest pounding as the words came out of Paw-paw's mouth. I don't know if it was the medication or the shock that made him not understand what the doctor was saying. I went to visit him almost every day after work. I would scold him for not getting out of bed. He would shake his head back and forth at me. I demanded that the nurse give him something to eat. How could he get stronger if he wasn't being fed? He begged for something to drink. I'd sit on the vinyl chair next to his bed as "Wheel of Fortune" began each afternoon. I hated the sound of that theme song and still do. Looking at him, I knew he was near death, but I couldn't accept it in my mind. He'd be out. He had to get out.

When he was put in ICU, I sat and watched him. I couldn't understand how someone I loved so much could have to endure such misery. Not to mention, the reality that he would one day be gone. The day I received the phone call that he died, I folded in half and sat in the hallway outside my classroom. I wanted to stay there on the floor.

It's funny how the world doesn't stop to share your loss. Sitting at a red light, I envisioned myself standing in the middle of the road with my arms out, screaming stop! He was one of the only people I bonded with as a child through adulthood, and he was gone. I wanted the world to acknowledge what I'd lost.

Chapter 34

One day, at the end of my third and last pregnancy, I was shopping for the new baby. My belly sticking out, only weeks before my due date. I stood at the wall of infant socks in Walmart, overwhelmed by the choices. Alone, I had already been to several other stores, loading up on newborn necessities. I noticed a woman standing to my left. Mumbling to herself, she seemed flustered with the choices of newborn socks. She looked towards me and smiled nervously. As she spoke, her eyes glazed over with tears.

"My daughter is having a girl. It's our first grandchild." Her joy and excitement caught me off guard. I admired the pride radiating from her expression.

"Oh, that is exciting." I smiled.

"What are you having?"

"A girl," I responded.

"When are you due? My daughter is due in three weeks."

"I'm due at about the same time," I replied.

She lit up with excitement for me. "Oh, is this your first?" She was giddy.

"No, my third." I smiled and made my way towards the opposite end of the wall.

"You're used to this, then," she gestured with her hand as if swatting her words away.

"Nah, you never get used to this." I laughed as I caressed my belly and walked away.

I couldn't stop thinking about how nice she was, and I loved seeing a mother excited to pick out socks for a granddaughter she'd never met. I wandered through the baby aisles. I fantasized about picking up the phone and calling my mom. While gripping the shopping cart, I closed my eyes and thought about what it would be like to have a conversation with her that didn't leave me exhausted. For a second, I imagined being able to depend on her to guide me through my choices and help me prepare to bring my child into the world. I wanted to pick up the phone and tell my dad how much my kids missed him. How we all missed him. I shook my head and opened my eyes to reality.

Suddenly, I had to find the woman I had just encountered. Something about her made me want to be near her, although I had no idea who she was. She beamed a motherly love I craved.

As I turned the corner, I saw her standing there, still carefully considering which socks to purchase. I quietly made my way back to her. With my cart beside her, tears filling my eyes, I whispered, "She's one lucky girl."

Epilogue

Recently, while out for breakfast I noticed a sign on the wall of the resteraunt that read,"Before I Die Wall" with an arrow pointing down the hall. I'd eaten breakfast there many times and never noticed the sign. As I turned the corner I saw a wall with the sentence starter written over and over "Before I die I want to _____".

Patrons used chalk to fill in the blanks. The first sentence I read said "**Before I die I want to** _write a book_." I hope the person who wrote that realizes all you have to do is write the "damn thing". Just get it out. Don't worry about the book being perfect, just write it. The odds of being picked up by a publisher are not great, but that should never keep a story from being written. We are in a time where self publishing is realistic and no one should feel their writing isn't good enough to share. Write the damn thing! Self publish it if you have to. Never think it will be easy. Writing, self publishing is a beast. Stay the course, it's worth it.

Expect disapproval and accept it if you are writing a memoir. People have their own version of events and ideas of what my reason was for writing this book. I have finally arrived in a place where I can look beyond those opinions and resonate in the idea that I had to write this for me.

If you are lucky readers will enjoy and connect to your story, whether it is fiction or nonfiction. There will also be readers who will not like your writing, that is ok too. Never let bad reviews discourage you from the desire to write, bad reviews are part of the process.

Also, be ready for people you've never met to have a connection to your story. This also caught me off guard, and at the same time has motivated me to continue to share my story. I have learned that to continue healing I can't keep it inside.

I wonder if things would have turned out differently for the people I love if they would have found a way to get it out instead of holding it all in. This story, my story, is not over with this book. There is more to come.

Made in the USA
Coppell, TX
25 March 2025

47533905R00079